Developing
and Promoting
Graphic Novel
Collections

Steve
Miller

Neal-Schuman Publishers, Inc.

New York   London

Published by Neal-Schuman Publishers, Inc.
100 William Street, Suite 2004
New York, NY 10038

The paper used in this publication meets the minimum requirements of American National
Standard for Information Sciences—Permanence of Paper for Printed Library Materials,
ANSI Z39.48-1992. ∞

Library of Congress Cataloging-in-Publication Data

Miller, Steve, 1969–
    Developing and promoting graphic novel collections / Steve Miller.
       p. cm. — (Teens @ the library series)
    Includes bibliographical references and index.
    ISBN 1–55570–461–1 (alk. paper)
    1. Libraries—Special collections—Graphic novels. 2. School libraries—Book
selection—United States—Handbooks, manuals, etc. 3. Young adults' libraries—Book
selection—United States—Handbooks, manuals, etc. 4. Graphic novels—United States.
5. Teenagers—Books and reading—United States. I. Title. II. Series.

Z692.G7M55 2005
025.2'89—dc22
                                      2004040159

Contents

Series Editor Foreword

Joel Shoemaker

This outstanding book by Steve (*not* the band) Miller is a message from the trenches, and the message is: Graphic novels are the hottest new thing in YA collections since . . . what, the Internet? The difference is that the technology that brought us the Internet is ubiquitous. Unless your library lacks electricity, chances are good that over the last couple of decades your library has been automated, hooked up to the Web, and has been providing various forms of electronic access to information for your patrons, including teens, for quite some time.

In contrast, some of us are still getting our feet wet building a graphic novel collection. Because of confusion over terminology, cataloging, and audience, among other things, individual librarians, library systems, and library consortia are only now finding that it is time to say, "Okay, let's order some graphic novels and see what happens."

Fortunately, Steve Miller, the author of *Developing and Promoting Graphic Novel Collections,* had the same experience. And thankfully, he got in early. In fact, he realized that there wasn't much information out there on the topic, and instead of bemoaning the fact, he decided to host two online electronic lists so that others going through the same things would not have such a hard time. As this thorough, interesting, and informative book reveals, Steve has found ways to share his many years of experience with the reader in such a way as to answer the questions you might have, whether you want to read this books sequentially, dip into it here and there for discussion of particular topics, or even read it Manga-style—back to front.

Mr. Miller provides the nuts and bolts of what this form is all about, including an overview of the relationships between graphic novels and their progenitors—cartoons, comic strips, and comics. Being responsive to our teen customers' needs and desires, he shows us how to use the graphic novel collection to assess further those needs and develop programs based on the interests of your particular teens. Certainly literacy is one of the foremost concerns of librarians today, and visual literacy—one important component of reading graphic novels—is becoming more important culture-wide as we consume ever increasing amounts of advertising, movies, videos, and so on.

Whether you are experienced or still poised on the edge, thinking that maybe the time has come for you to begin developing a graphic novel collection, you will find that, like all the books in the Teens @ the Library series, this book:

- draws from the best and most current research.
- targets the changing needs of today's teenagers.
- cites the most innovative models.
- provides practical suggestions that have been real-world tested.
- calls on each of us to realize the highest ideals of our profession.

If *Developing and Promoting Graphic Novel Collections* were listed in a course catalog, it might be called, "A Brief History of Graphic Novels." But it could also be known as, "Graphic Novels and Teens: Make the Connection," "Graphic Novels in Your Library," and "Graphic Novel Appreciation." In addition, it provides one-stop shopping for invaluable online resources, vendors, and sources from which you can continue to learn about this new and important area of interest. By starting with this book and using the tools Mr. Miller recommends, you can stay in touch and up to date. You probably already know how rabid some of your teen patrons are about graphic novels—read this book to learn what you can do to continue to promote a vital and varied collection that builds on their enthusiastic interest.

Preface

Developing and Promoting Graphic Novel Collections is a primer for librarians and educators that builds a familiarity with a unique and popular form of storytelling. It explains what graphic novels are, how libraries can bring this format to users, how public and school libraries can develop quality collections, and how to market and program with these materials.

More than just a collection development guide, this is a handbook not only for librarians who are interested in starting a graphic novel collection but also for those who already have a collection and are looking to maximize its use and importance. *Developing and Promoting Graphic Novel Collections* is both a starting place and a resource that can be consulted again and again.

COMICS AND GRAPHIC NOVELS

Comic books have been a part of American culture since the 1930s, when the first rag-pulp superheroes were born. Initially dismissed as "kid stuff," the monthly issues of *Superman* and *Batman* have evolved into today's most dynamic literary format: the graphic novel. Graphic novels, simply, are stories expressed through both text and artwork. While illustrated novels use art to *enhance* the text, the pictures in graphic novels are as integral to the story as the words themselves.

No longer thirty pages of *biff!, bam!, bop!,* contemporary titles explore, through original stories and artwork, modern themes like racism, social change, romance, and drama. There are still the classic favorites that revive the superheroes of DC and Marvel—now presenting in one volume storylines that once took dozens of issues to unfold—as well as new cult favorites, including the popular new Manga titles based on successful Japanese film and television characters.

Quality graphic novels contain complex storylines and literary styles that elevate them to the level of literature. While many titles are still rooted in science fiction and fantasy, others might more appropriately be classified as realism, history, or even biography. Graphic novels have even taken on the literary canon; *Doctor Jekyll & Mr. Hyde, The Scarlet Letter, Beowulf, Don Quixote,* and many more have been beautifully adapted to the format.

LIBRARIES AND GRAPHIC NOVELS

The primary focus of public and school libraries is to bring information to patrons. Graphic novels—because of their diverse and dynamic content—can increase literacy, understanding, and library use among even reluctant or low-level readers. They also expand the content available to visual-spatial and visual-linguistic learners. Illustrated aspects can fill in the blanks of key concepts for "picture" learners who may not be able to glean them from the actual text of the novel. All around, graphic novels provide access to a full range of literary and recreational genres in a format that young students and reluctant readers find appealing.

Graphic novels provide one more tool for libraries to reach their audience of users and one more method by which librarians and educators can build reading skills in young learners.

READING AND USING *DEVELOPING AND PROMOTING GRAPHIC NOVEL COLLECTIONS*

Chapter 1, "Exploring Graphic Novels," has three sections to maximize librarians' understanding of this popular new format. *Categories* defines the graphic novel format and explains its place in the context of comic art. *Evolution* traces the long route from pulp-comic kid stuff to sophisticated, quality texts suitable for library collections. This section also looks ahead to future popularity and trends in graphic novels. *Genres* explores the diversity of subjects, both fiction and nonfiction, encompassed by graphic novels.

Chapter 2, "Graphic Novels in Libraries," looks at four key elements to getting graphic novels onto the shelves, making them accessible, and keeping them in the collection. *Collection Development* provides a "Five Cs" model—credibility, circulation, commitment, collection, and cost—for selecting the best materials for a library's community and offers tips for making the case to managers and other decision makers. *Acquisition* reveals the methods and outlets through which graphic novels are made available, including local stores and standard vendors. *Cataloging* offers approaches to organizing the materials, making them available to appropriate age levels, and properly describing them in the catalog. Lastly, *Collection Maintenance and Defense* gives practical advice for dealing with vandalism, wear, and challenges to materials as well as strategies for shelving and weeding out materials.

Chapter 3, "Promoting Graphic Novels," offers three avenues for getting materials into readers' hands. *Marketing* explains how libraries can promote graphic collections within the library and to the larger community. *Programming* looks at four distinct types of programs—discussion groups, book talks, contests and activities, and speakers and presenters—and offers suggestions and plans for implementing them in the library. *Education* reveals the potential for linking graphic novels with critical thinking skills, language and literature study, and classroom initiatives.

Chapter 4, "Core Titles Listing," presents the author's picks for all levels of collection. The recommendations are divided into: *Starting Out,* for libraries that have no graphic novels and want to test-market a collection; *Small and Growing,* for expanding the use, value, and quality of an emerging collection; and *Titles Every Collection "Should" Have,* a compilation of titles that showcases the breadth and diversity of the format.

Chapter 5, "Finding the Best of Graphic Novels," helps librarians locate lists of best-sellers, resources and suggested readings for keeping current and provides contact information for publishers.

This book presents accepted practice, fresh ideas, and a clear explanation of *what* graphic novels are, providing a stable foundation on which librarians and educators can build. *Developing and Promoting Graphic Novel Collections* grounds its knowledge in journal articles from the past ten years, the online archive of the Graphic Novels in Libraries e-mail list, and the author's discussions with teachers and librarians. *Developing and Promoting Graphic Novel Collections* helps build a librarian's confidence to discuss and work with this unique form of storytelling.

Acknowledgments

Thanks go to Faye, Cathy, Lowell, and Carin, and to the members and supporters of The Graphic Novels in Libraries e-mail discussion group, a regular source of inspiration and practicality.

1

Exploring Graphic Novels

1.1 CATEGORIES

Graphic novels are part of a larger family of comic art. The culmination of a long history, these books blend artwork and text to create a unique method of storytelling that is very appealing to children and teenagers.

1

1.1.1 What Are Graphic Novels?

Graphic novels are stories told in a comics format that express a continuous tale. The art is what brings dimension and flavor to the story, bringing the dialogue and narrative to life. This visual layer of the story can improve the reader's appreciation and understanding of the narration and dialogue. Unlike regular novels, which rely on text alone, the images in graphic novels enhance and reinforce the movement of the story. This is what makes graphic novels unique—the joining of drawings and text is fundamental. Neither element can tell the story alone.

Comic books use art and text in the same way, but they express a storyline in short installments rather than in a single book. Each issue generally ends in a cliffhanger that entices the reader to acquire the next episode. These serials can take years to tell a complex story, with subplots interspersed along the way. Publishers often print issues related to a particular storyline together to create a bound collection. This thick comic book is then released as a graphic novel.

One way to think of it is to consider a comic book as a form of serial fiction, with its single chapters published in monthly magazines. While not in the comic-art format, these text-based installments could be gathered and reprinted in a single book. This is equivalent to a bound collection of comic books. True graphic novels, in the strictest sense, are usually single, full-length stories told through comic art. Whether a collection of reprinted comic books or an original story, the result is a long story told in comic art: a graphic novel. Another way to think of it is to consider bound collections of comic books as a book of short stories and a graphic novel as a full-length novel. In actual practice, however, bound collections are considered graphic novels, despite there being semantic differences between the two.

Graphic novels (often abbreviated GNs) can be seen as the natural evolution of comic books. They entertain us with longer, richer, and more detailed stories in a single book. This allows the comic art to grow to its full potential, unfettered by artificial breaks in the story caused by monthly installments.

Comic art is a unique storytelling method that uses text and images to express the mood and action of a story. These draw the reader into the story *visually*. Just like a text-based book, comics require active participation by the reader. With a graphic novel, however, the reader must make inferences and associations between the words and the pictures in order to understand the story. From an educational viewpoint, this can be a benefit.

In 1985, Will Eisner, one of the first creators of graphic novels, wrote *Comics and Sequential Art*. Known as the "father of American graphic novels," Eisner was the first to coin the term *sequential art* to describe comics. In sequential art, the stories are told through a series of panels containing art and text that, when read in sequence, express narrative action. This definition works for comic strips, comic books, and graphic novels.

> **The term graphic novel *is often abbreviated as GN (plural, GNs).***

What Is Special about Comic Books and Graphic Novels?

The text and images work together to express the mood and action of the story. These draw the reader into the story visually. Just like a text-based book, comics require active participation by the reader, but they also require the reader to make inferences and associations between the words and the pictures.

1.1.2 What Makes Them Graphic?

Graphic novels are so named because of the comic art that is used to tell the story. This form of comic art is considered graphic because the illustrations are integral to the story. Some literary novels contain illustrations and use the images to supplement the story, but these novels can be understood without the pictures. The illustrations are nice but not required.

This is not so with comic art and, in particular, graphic novels. If the images are removed from comic art, the remaining text does not convey the story. The inverse is also true. If the text is removed, leaving only panels of artwork, the images must be carefully woven in order to present the entire message. Both the pictures and the words provide essential cues to interpreting the story. "Silent," i.e., without text, comic art can be a tricky thing to understand! Although they are not common, wordless graphic novels do exist, most notably in the works of Richard Delgado (*Age of Reptiles*) and Masashi Tanaka (*Gon*).

Graphic novels have suffered a certain stigma because of their name. To someone inexperienced with this form of storytelling, a reasonable first impression would be to assume that graphic novels are *explicit*. That is frequently the first, and incorrect, impression. Unfortunately, when graphic novels were born in the late 1970s and early 1980s, there was also a rise in the amount of sexual comic material being produced. This confused the public, who did not understand that a graphic novel is based on its graphic arts and illustration, rather than being a sexually explicit novel. *Heavy Metal* magazine, for example, was an adult illustrated fantasy periodical that used comic art to express violence, sexuality, and social commentary. Not all comic art was for children! This type of artistic expression, while appropriate for adults, contributed to the reputation of certain comic art being explicit.

In any market, whether cinematic or bibliographic, companies distribute what sells. Books, movies, and graphic novels are available for a wide variety of ages and interests. While there is a market for adult-oriented material, today's graphic novel market is blossoming with books for children and teens. Adult content, however, does not often appear in comic books. The comic book arena, especially among mainstream publishers such as DC and Marvel, remains teen-friendly and kid-safe.

A more apt term for graphic novel, and one certainly less connotative, is *comic novel*. Just as a comic book is a short book of comic art, a comic novel is a longer book of comic art. Many libraries avoid the issue of negative connotation by using the name "Comic Novels" to describe their collection. This label is often used when library collections are located in youth or teen areas. It also helps educate patrons about the differences between a flimsy comic book and a more substantial comic novel. While the term *comic novel* is a good middle ground in the battle for respectability, it promotes the perception that *comic* connotes *humorous*, which is not always the case. In the case of comic art, *comic* refers to the form, not the content of the story.

> **Remember: Not all graphic novels are explicit,**
> **and not all comics are funny.**

1.1.3 Anatomy of a Comic

Comic art is a sequential progression of images, combined with text, that convey information. Comic art contains four basic elements: panels, gutters, balloons, and text. Panels provide space for the artwork. Balloons allow words to be inserted. Gutters provide strips of empty space between the panels. Text brings language to the story.

Examine the following comic to see how these four elements of comic art work together with a border and motion lines to create a simple comic strip.

The (Very) Accidental Comic.   by Steve Miller

The (Very) Accidental Comic.

PANELS

A single frame of a comic is a *panel*. The art is drawn within the panels. The shape and size of the panels can add dimension to the story, emphasizing mood or theme.

Comic strips often use box shapes to frame each panel. With their limited length of three to five panels, these boxes give comic strips a consistent, simple format from one frame to the next. They also aid the reader by breaking the sequence into visually separate areas.

Comic books, on the other hand, have entire pages in which to lay out the panels. Dialogue and development scenes frequently use squares arranged in a linear fashion (a box-box-box approach). Action sequences can fill a page with several oversized, angular frames. To show speed and intensity in a comic book, the layout of frames on a page might have a "shattered" appearance, where each "shard" shows character reactions or multiple points of view to an important event. Quite often, the layout of a page is, in itself, as artistic and creative as the drawings made inside the individual panels. Sometimes a single panel can fill the entire page.

A sequence of box panels in any comic art story is read sequentially, from left to right. This sequential art shows movement of the characters and story. In book-length comics—both comic books and graphic novels—full-page action layouts can be interpreted as a single moment in time. In other words, a sequence of panels can explore a few characters in progressive moments, or it can display multiple characters or events concurrently in a single moment.

In The (Very) Accidental Comic some license was taken. The narrative panels at the beginning and end are traditional boxes while the middle panel is a trapezoid angled in the direction of the character's motion. This is intended to emphasize the movement of the character on his uphill journey. Some comic art may rely on page layout, rather than gutters, to organize the panels. Gutters may or may not be required.

Comics are Read in the Direction That the Language Is Read

Japanese comics are read backwards from an English speaker's point of view. They are read from back to front, right to left, top to bottom. When these books are released in an English-speaking country, the order of the pages is not always reversed. Therefore, the speech balloons may contain English words, but the pages retain the Japanese sequence. Japanese graphic novels, or Manga, may initially confuse readers who are unfamiliar with this practice.

GUTTERS

The *gutter* is the space between the panels. Gutters do more than delineate the panels; they provide a psychological resting spot, an indication to the reader that something is changing. When reading from one panel to another across a gutter, the characters, scenes, times, and points of view can change.

Gutters can also be seen as the punctuation of comic art. If the scene or time changes, the pause can be perceived as a period. If the characters continue a thought from one panel to the next, the gutter could be interpreted as a comma. Some panels can have a "punch line" in the middle, with a final comment or rebuttal in the last panel. In this case, the gutter after the joke might be seen as an exclamation point.

Scott McCloud, author of *Understanding Comics,* analogizes this blank space as the "nothingness" of an eye blink. When the reader's eye moves between two panels, the reader's mind attempts to relate the two scenes and unconsciously fill in the blanks to explain what has happened to the characters during the pause.

Notice how, in the middle panel of The (Very) Accidental Comic, Smiley seems farther away than in the other two panels. The blank space between the panel gives the artist an opportunity to change the reader's point of view. This reveals more of Smiley's environment and places emphasis on the hill he is trying to climb.

BALLOONS

A *balloon,* or speech bubble, is the element in which the words spoken by the characters are written. Balloons can use shape, color, and type style to indicate the intensity, mood, or volume of a speaker. The style of a balloon is like the adverb of the speech. For example, a balloon drawn with a jagged bottom that looks like icicles, with text rendered in jagged lines, is akin to the character making a statement "icily." Large balloons with bold, capital letters indicates "loudly." Square balloons with angular letters are frequently used to indicate the speech of a mechanism, such as a computer. Not all comic art uses balloons. Sometimes the text is written near the speaker's head.

In The (Very) Accidental Comic, Smiley is making a simple statement in the first panel. The reader can notice this from the friendly, rounded edges of his speech balloon and from the "pointer" beneath the balloon. Pointers indicate which character is speaking.

In the middle panel, the shape of the balloon changes from straight lines to a cloud. Instead of an angled, direct pointer, small circles emanate from Smiley's head. These changes indicate that the character is thinking, rather than speaking.

In the final panel, Smiley is back to speaking again with a standard, rounded balloon, but this time the letters are capitalized. This adds energy to his phrase and indicates that the character is excited or emphatic.

TEXT

More than a means to convey thoughts, words and letters are often part of the artwork in a comic. Cues to the speaker's location and mood are revealed in the way the letters are rendered. *Text* in comic art can express not only information but also a mood. For example, letters made of large, jagged lines can indicate a character speaking in a loud voice. Wavy or curly letters could mean a character is speaking affectionately—or is, indeed, underwater.

In the first panel of The (Very) Accidental Comic, Smiley's speech is in a standard "handwriting" typeface. The words "avoid" and "pitfall" are emphasized to draw attention to the key words of the speech. Notice that in the middle panel, the letters change to small, dense, italicized type. This reinforces a sense of motion in that panel, and it emphasizes distance. In the final panel, Smiley is speaking with capitalized letters. This shows that he is excited or shouting. Again, emphasis is added to the beginning of his speech by displaying the letters in bold type.

As an exercise in comics literacy, try reading Smiley's comic without looking at the words. Can his actions be interpreted the same way? If the images are covered and only the text is read, is the perception of the story the same?

BORDERS

Most comic art makes use of a *border* that separates it from the rest of the page. This encloses the strip and makes it easier to read.

MOTION LINES

Because comic art is a static medium, the illusion of movement is created through *motion lines* near a character. Characters are depicted ahead of the motion lines, with the lines trailing behind them, much as a wake follows a moving boat. The length of a motion line indicates the distance traveled. The quantity of lines can indicate the speed. The shape of the lines indicates the path traveled.

In the middle panel of The (Very) Accidental Comic, Smiley is drawn to the right of three lines. This indicates that he is moving rapidly to the right, in this case, uphill.

The elements of comic art can be put together in many ways. The number of panels, their layout on a page, and the number of pages in the item determine the type of material being read. The comic art family has four manifestations: cartoons, comic strips, comic books, and graphic novels. It is almost as if visual storytellers started with the quick sketches and cutting social commentary of editorial cartoons only to find that more space was needed to express themselves. Comic strips then developed, allowing the latitude of multiple panels and daily strips. More ideas and stories could be expressed in this form. See **5.2: Comic Art Glossary** for more information.

As comic strips became more popular with the public and as artists and storytellers became more experienced, strips began to develop regular characters and storylines. Gradually, the idea of filling small magazines with color artwork developed. These new comic books gave plenty of room to express story, mood, and action while still keeping with the episodic tradition of comic strips.

In the latter part of the twentieth century, however, even that was not enough. Artists who had grown up and been raised on comic books wanted to use comic art in even more innovative ways. The graphic novel was born. Just like text-based stories, tales told in comic art can span hundreds of pages.

1.1.4 Summary

- Comic art varies in complexity.
- Comic art uses visual and text elements to relate a story.
- There are four types of comic art.

1.2 EVOLUTION

Most people are familiar with the comics that appear as strips in daily news-papers and the monthly magazines filled with superheroes. The image of comic art as poor quality, read-and-toss kid's stuff is rapidly fading. While there are some cheaply produced publications in existence, modern printing and coloring methods, as well as better paper, have improved the appearance and usability of the printed product. Nor are comics, in any format, just for children. There has been a wide variety of adult material available for many years. Some of this material, however, was responsible for giving a negative connotation to the "graphic" in graphic novels in the minds of the public.

Comics, especially in the form of the graphic novel, have finally attained a new respectability and sophistication in the eyes of the public and the pub-lishing world. They have been used for both entertainment and education, with subjects ranging from classic literature, humor, and original stories to nonfiction documentary and political statements. Literary works, such as *Macbeth* and *The Scarlet Letter*, have been adapted to comic art. This visual interpretation gives readers an opportunity to experience the mood and themes of classic literature in an easy-to-read format. A picture can truly be worth a thousand words!

From the nineteenth century to the twenty-first century, the comic evolved from woodcuts with narrative to the glossy-paged graphic novel we have to-day. Even now, the medium continues to grow as artists explore comics on the World Wide Web.

Since the 1980s, after throwing off the negative image of its convulsive history, graphic novels have proven to appeal to the general public and even scholarly tastes. Since the 1990s, graphic novels have continued to evolve in their mainstream appeal. Libraries and educators were among the first to dis-cover their merit as legitimate publications with literary and educational value. This respectability was aided by a new sophistication in the subject matter and artwork developed by graphic novel writers and artists. Ever eager to expand their markets, contemporary graphic novel distributors are focus-ing on material appropriate for libraries.

Here is a short history of comic art. This brief overview will provide some basic ideas and show how comics have changed through time.

1.2.1 Infancy: Caveman to 1900

Credit for the earliest sequential art in history goes to unknown artists of the Paleolithic period. Cave paintings depict men preparing for a hunt, chasing animals, and bringing home the quarry for dinner. More than static artwork, this series of images work together to tell a story. These ancient pictures fit a loose, prewriting definition of comics.

The Egyptians take second billing in comic history. Many of their engravings accurately show entire scenes from daily life. One piece in particular shows farmers planting grain, overseers supervising a harvest, millers grinding, cooks baking, and a member of the royal house eating bread. Hieroglyphs (Egyptian text) throughout the engraving explain the amount of grain produced and the quantity received in taxes and extol the honor of the royal family. Here, again, is a series of images that use words to elaborate the picture.

Early American native cultures, such as the Aztecs and Mayans, also used this type of artwork to educate and inform their citizens. This early comic art often documented ceremonial or official duties.

While certainly not humorous, early comics and sequential art were an extension of artwork that communicated facts about many civilizations. More interesting, however, is recent comics history: The 1900s—a hundred years of comics.

1.2.2 Childhood: The Golden Age of the 1930s

Before the 1700s, drawings and paintings unintentionally contained comic art. That is, any sequential images depicted in art were there for functional reasons. Comic art was not used for its own sake. In the 1700s and 1800s, artists began to explore the nuances of this progression of images. It was at this time that shifting points of view, multiple characters, and actual stories began to blossom.

By the early 1900s, mass-produced visual artwork began moving from circulars and flyers to bound material.

In 1929, the Belgian artist Hergé (Georges Remi) began writing the adventures of Tintin, a roving boy-reporter. Praised as the creator of the "clear line" style, Hergé's twenty-four volumes are still available as graphic novels.

Stellar Comics!

Hergé's work was so influential that the Belgian Astronomical Society named a planetoid after him. Discovered in 1953, Planet Hergé is in the asteroid belt between Mars and Jupiter.

Comic art evolved in America as well. Moving from single panels to comic strips, publishers of the 1930s were including comic art in daily newspapers.

The *Tarzan* stories by Edgar Rice Burroughs were illustrated and turned into comic strips. Phillip Nowlan's stories were also adapted and became the *Buck Rogers in the 25th Century* A.D. comic strip. By the end of the 1930s, newspaper comics were graced with *Dick Tracy* and *Flash Gordon.*

This was also the birth of the comic book in America. Publishers looking for new ways to expand their market took on jobs reprinting comic strips in a bound format. One of the first among these, the experimental comic book *Funnies on Parade,* caught on and showed the publishing world the market for comics.

By transforming these works of prose fiction into comic art and by binding disparate strips into a single book, the early glimmers of what was to become graphic novels appeared.

Super Sales!

Two boys from Cleveland, Ohio, created a blue-costumed alien with amazing powers. They sold the rights to a New York comics publisher for less than $150, and Action Comics #1 *debuted in 1938 with its new hero, Superman.*

More and more heroes were created, and readers of the 1930s and 1940s demanded even more adventures. This was the Golden Age of Comics.

Things changed after World War II. A new genre was on the rise: True Crime, featuring stories about criminals, outlaws, and bad guys. In the late 1940s and early 1950s, horror comics began to appear, such as *Crypt of Terror* and *Vault of Horror.* These were rapidly followed by a wave of science fiction comic books, along with the classic image of "pulp comics"—scantily clad, voluptuous women. The post-war era also saw the birth of illustrated classics. Comic art adaptations of literary works such as *The Three Musketeers* and *Wuthering Heights* were popular.

1.2.3 Adolescence: Post-War to 1970

American comics culture came to an abrupt precipice in 1953 when Frederic Wertham, a child psychologist, published *Seduction of the Innocent.* In it, he detailed seven years of research on "juvenile delinquents" and concluded that crime comic books were to blame. Wertham demanded that action be taken before another generation of young people were ruined. Although not a best-selling book, his crusade against comic books reached national attention with a 1954 article in *Reader's Digest,* "Comic Books: Blueprints for Delinquency." The resulting hysteria over the evils of comic books reached kitchen tables and PTAs across the country.

A U.S. Senate committee took up the banner and launched its own investigation into comic books and juvenile delinquency. The committee established no connection between them, but the publishers banded together to fight the negative publicity. They created the Comic Magazine Association of America (CMAA).

In an effort to demonstrate the comic industry's responsibility to its readers, the CMAA created the Comics Code Authority (CCA). This effort at self-regulation, adopted in 1954, provided standards for editorial matter and advertising content that would guide the comic book industry for the next forty years. To be eligible to earn the seal of approval of the CCA, a comic had to demonstrate responsibility in many areas, including:

- The content could not have scenes or instruments associated with "walking dead, torture, vampires, ghouls, cannibalism, and werewolfism."
- Dialogue had to contain proper grammar and no vulgarities.
- Ridicule of religion was prohibited.
- Costume design was standardized, no suggestive poses were allowed, and females could not be drawn with exaggerated physical characteristics.
- Portrayals of marriage and sex could not treat divorce as desirable, show violence or love scenes, and could not promote disrespect for parents, the moral code, or honorable behavior.
- Advertising of liquor, tobacco, knives, fireworks, and gambling were proscribed.
- The only medical, health, or toiletry ads allowed were those endorsed by the American Medial Association or the American Dental Association.

The results of the Senate committee and the regulatory action of the CMAA could not offset the public outcry against comics. Much like a teenager reprimanded by a parent, comic book sales in America slumped into an almost adolescent depression throughout the 1950s and 1960s. Sales did not rise again until Marvel Comics and DC Comics reenergized the medium in the 1970s.

The U.S. Government Got into Comics!

In the 1950s, the Social Security Administration used comic books to educate Americans about social security benefits. Titles included Social Security for Farm Families *and* John's First Job.

While American comics were experiencing a turbulent period, European comic artists were thriving. Two major artists reached the worldwide comics scene, with their work translated into many languages and reprinted in bound collections. French writer René Goscinny and French artist Albert Uderzo created *Asterix the Gaul* in 1959. In 1957, Belgian artist Pierre Culliford brought forth characters called *Les Schtroumpfs*. His works were later adapted to animation and, with a quick name change, Peyo's *Smurfs* became recognized around the world.

In Japan, comic art was having its own growth spurt. A unique artistic style and storytelling method, which became known as Manga, was being developed. One influential artist, Osamu Tezuka, adapted Robert Louis Stevenson's *Treasure Island* in 1947. His *New Treasure Island* became a bestseller. On the heels of World War II, the book overcame the decimation of Japan's morale to sell over 400,000 copies. Nineteen-year-old Tezuka created the seeds of a new way of looking at comics and authored many popular works, such as *Astro Boy*, until his death in 1989. Prior to World War II, comics in Japan were seen as something for children. By the 1960s, a rising student movement embraced the Manga comic style. Manga continued to grow and diversify in the 1980s, encompassing a great variety of subjects, from jokes to melodrama, science fiction to travelogues, education manuals to simple humor.

An international hit! By 1996, René Goscinny's Asterix stories sold over 280 million copies worldwide!

Comics Firsts!

The first standard for American comics was the Comic Code Authority (CCA), created in 1954 by the Comic Magazine Association of America. It guided the hands of comic artists for more than forty years. By the late 1990s, however, only DC Comics and Archie Comics continued to use the CCA seal of approval.

The 1960s saw the first animated television series become popular in Japan and America. The characters of Astro Boy, Gigantor, and Speed Racer took root in both cultures. Japan, however, was unique in its treatment of graphic novels. Their animation and comics industries were, and still are, very tightly united. Animated television series and movies would be released and then drawn as comic books, just as popular comics books inevitably became animated.

In 1970s America, comic books were coming out of their decline. Marvel Comics and DC Comics revitalized the field with new heroes, often organized into teams. This allowed greater flexibility with storytelling—instead of a sequential story about one hero, several characters of the team could be sent on different missions. Storylines became more complex, often interwoven throughout many issues. While still ending with a cliffhanger, monthly comics became part of a "never-ending saga." The richer storylines contributed to the resurgence of American comics in the 1970s and 1980s.

During this time, an underground comics movement was growing, created by nonmainstream publishers. Many of these independent comic publishing houses focused on adult markets, providing a wide array of fiction through their comic art. One popular adult illustrated fantasy magazine was *Heavy Metal,* which was created in France in the mid-1970s. While the "voluptuous space vixen" had found a home, not all underground publications were erotic.

By the mid-1970s, there were two viable markets—comics for kids and illustrated material for adults. Some adult comics, as with books published today, contained suggestive or intentionally erotic material. There were also, however, original, nonerotic fiction stories for adults being created. The first acknowledged graphic novel came in 1978. Will Eisner, now regarded as the father of American graphic novels, created *A Contract with God.* This book was held in such high esteem that when the comics industry created an award for excellence in comic art, they called it the Eisner Award.

Comics Firsts!

The first American graphic novel was A Contract with God, *written by Will Eisner in 1978.*

1.2.4 Maturity: 1970 to 1990

Creative writers in the 1980s followed Eisner's suit, breathing new life into comic books. Original graphic novels were born.

What was so special about Graphic Novels? Their longer narrative were suitable to building characters and scenes that could be more complex than those found in monthly comic books. By placing an entire story within one book, comic art could convey a sense of dramatic tension and atmosphere. This was a significant leap forward for comic art. A new market was discovered—people wanted to read "feature-length" comics! These books, billed as "graphic novels," were often superior to comics. Unlike pulp comic books, graphic novels were printed on higher-grade paper with higher-quality printing. Comics enthusiasts celebrated. No longer would there be any waiting for the next installment, no more missed issues that could be hard to acquire! The entire story was in one book.

In 1985, Will Eisner gave readers an insider's view of the comic art philosophy. *Comics and Sequential Art* explained not only the how-to, but also the why-for of the art form.

With an increase in the respectable reviews for comic material, bookstores and libraries began carrying graphic novels in the late 1980s. This was a cue for mainstream book publishers to enter the fray. Publishers, frantic to catch the GN wave, began to produce a handful of individual comics for the express purpose of subsequently reprinting them as a graphic novel.

At this point in comic history, the comics-publishing industry felt too restricted by the CCA. Observing that American culture had changed over the almost forty since its inception, publishers began backing out of the CCA. By the end of the twentieth century, only a handful of companies still endorsed it.

In 1987 and 1992, Art Spiegelman created his two-part epic story of one man's experience during the Holocaust. *Maus: A Survivor's Tale* was a milestone in the history of comics because it was one of the first original biographic graphic novels. Originally serialized, it was its form as a graphic novel that received media acclaim. Spiegelman received that 1992 Pulitzer Prize for Literature for his work on *Maus*—the first cartoonist to be so honored.

The media was not alone in their accolades. Comic art had been receiving the attention of scholars for some time. Two notable comic art collections are the Michigan State University's Comic Art Collection and the Cartoon Research Library at Ohio State University (OSU). OSU's collection is noteworthy for its Will Eisner Collection and its Manga Collection, which it began developing in 1998.

By the 1990s, a substantial quantity of all Japanese publishing was devoted to Manga, with sales in the billions of dollars per year. With unmatched attention to process, Japanese publishers devised a highly efficient mechanism to focus their work: Large magazines were created that printed the stories as installments, sometimes as short as two or three pages each. When a story proved to be popular, a higher-quality, longer version was printed.

Comic Firsts!

Maus: A Survivor's Tale, *by Art Spiegelman, was the first graphic novel to win a major award. It received the 1992 Pulitzer Prize for Literature!*

Back in America, Scott McCloud followed up on Will Eisner's work with his 1993 pragmatically thorough *Understanding Comics.* An authoritative work to help bring noncomics readers up to speed about the medium, he brought together the best bits and explained the basics of not only the mechanics of the art form, but also the psychology of comics literacy. This work earned McCloud the title of "comics theorist."

Understanding Comics, by Scott McCloud, is a recommended must-have for any librarian who works with graphic novels or comics. It offers theories about how comic art is perceived in readers' minds.

Comics Firsts!

Barefoot Gen *was the first Japanese Manga to be translated into English. It later became anime-ted.*

In the late 1990s, sales of Manga accounted for almost half of Japan's book and magazine sales, topping $7 billion each year!

A foto novella, *a small comic book about 4 × 7 inches, is easy to carry. In Mexico, thousands are printed each week. It is estimated that one-third of the population of Mexico's 80 million people read this type of literature.* (Harvest of Life Web site, 2001)

1.2.5 The Present: 1990 to Today

Public libraries began taking a serious look at graphic novels in the 1980s and 1990s. Here is a quick recap of the last decade of the twentieth century, looking at journal and periodical articles that featured articles concerning graphic novels in public and school libraries.

This survey of professional library-related journals, done by the author in February 2003, shows a few interesting points:

- 63 percent of the references came from three sources: *Publisher's Weekly, School Library Journal,* and *Library Journal.*
- More articles about graphic novels were published in 2002 than were published in the five years before.
- More references to graphic novels were made in professional journals during the first two months of 2003 than were made in 1995, 1996, 1997, and 1998 combined.

Publishing industry and library journals were not the only sources featuring articles about graphic novels. In the 1990s and early 2000s, Graphic novel news turned up in *Newsweek, The New York Times, USA Today, The Wall Street Journal,* NPR's *All Things Considered, Journal of Adolescent & Adult Literacy, English Journal, Educational Resource Information Center* (ERIC), *Journal of Art & Design Education,* and many local newspapers around the country.

To illustrate the rapidly growing professional interest in graphic novels, consider the highlights of the last decade.

Public librarians began to think more about graphic novels when Keith R. A. DeCandido's article "Picture This: Graphic Novels in Libraries" appeared in *Library Journal* in March 1990. Ahead of its time, DeCandido's article began with, "Not many libraries have discovered graphic novels yet. The *American Heritage Dictionary* has not discovered graphic novels yet either; it does not define the term." (Two years after DeCandido's addressing of this dearth, however, *Maus* won the Pulitzer Prize for Literature.)

In the mid-1990s, *Voice of Youth Advocates* began to include quarterly columns of graphic novel reviews under the watchful eye of Kat Kan. *Voice of Youth Advocates* and *School Library Journal* were the first library journals to embrace the idea that graphic novels could be useful for librarians. Lora Bruggeman came through in *School Library Journal's* "Zap! Whoosh! Kerplow!" *School Library Journal* christened a brave new age for libraries interested in GNs. Following up with GN reviews by Betsy Levine and Francisca Goldsmith in 1998, *School Library Journal* began charting the waters and driving this trend.

In the summer of 1998, Michael R. Lavin, always striving for comprehensiveness, came through when *Serials Review* published, "Comic Books and Graphic Novels for Libraries: What to Buy?"

Articles and columns about graphic novels were steady throughout most of 1999. The reviews continued as more and more libraries explored which GNs to buy. It was not until that autumn that interest began to pick up again. The e-mail discussion list, Graphic Novels in Libraries (GNLIB-L), was created in October, and *Time* magazine published its cover story "Amazing Anime" in November of that year.

By the time the 1990s ended, Manga was rapidly moving into the public mainstream. Comics aficionados and librarians had more help than had been believed possible—some solid advice on starting GN collections, sources of regular reviews, a first insight into the industry, and a ready supply of answers simply an e-mail message away. The birth pains of "graphic novel librarianship" were over, but the best was yet to come.

In 2000, after two years of watching others review graphic novels, *Publisher's Weekly* began to seriously cover news of the comics industry. A year later, in an effort to help bookstores (and, unknowingly, libraries), *Publisher's Weekly* and Jessica Abel talked about "The Art of Selling Graphic Novels" in June 2001. Librarians lucky enough to catch it received sound advice on how to successfully market and display these new additions to their collections.

2002 will be remembered as the year when ideas about GNs in libraries really began to solidify. Recognizing that the field was coming into its own, Stephen Weiner, author of several books and articles on graphic novel collecting, led the way in *Library Journal*'s February issue with "Beyond Superheroes: Comics Get Serious."

By the spring of 2002, public and school libraries were established as players in the comics industry. "Graphic Novels Feel the Love," by Douglas Wolk in May's *Publisher's Weekly,* focused the response of publishers and distributors that had been tailoring services to this new comics market. Wolk and *Publisher's Weekly* showed that lightning can strike twice by including "The Manga Are Coming" in that same issue.

By this time, *Voice of Youth Advocates, School Library Journal,* and now *Publisher's Weekly* were making sure that almost every calendar month supplied librarians with reviews of current and classic graphic novels. Librarians across America had just enough time to read the articles about something called a "graphic novel collection" before attending the American Library Association's (ALA) summer conference, with its special preconference workshops about graphic novels.

Like putting out a fire with gasoline, the ALA kept interest alive by announcing that graphic novels would be the theme of Teen Read Week 2002. This caused a tumult of articles and discussions as librarians leapt to meet this new challenge in young adult librarianship. *School Library Journal* once again rose to dominate with their August issue, stocked with many GN-related articles beneath the cover story of "A Core Collection of Graphic Novels." "What Teens Want," by Michele Gorman, "No Flying, No Tights," by Walter Minkel, and "Graphic Novels, Seriously," by Evan St. Lifer all worked in harmony to bring graphic novels "out" for public and school librarians around the world.

In late 2002, *Library Journal,* a solid voice of reason in the library world, decided that graphic novels were no longer just a fad and asked Steve Raiteri to jump into the fray with a regular column of reviews.

At the end of 2002, *Booklist* and *Book Report* were getting in on the game. In the last *Book Report* issue of the year, Maureen Mooney moved beyond mere lists and into more philosophical issues with her "Graphic Novels: How They Can Work in Libraries." Calvin Reid and Heidi MacDonald became the names to watch in *Publisher's Weekly* in the last days of 2002, with their articles on "ibook" graphic novels and Manga. MacDonald summed it all up with her December article, claiming that 2002 was "The Year of the Graphic Novel."

Little more than ten years after Keith DeCandido bemoaned the sad state of graphic novels, the *American Heritage Dictionary* added "graphic novel" to its lexicon.

Top Professional Journals to Watch for Graphic Novel Reviews and News
1. *Voice of Youth Advocates* 2. *School Library Journal* 3. *Publisher's Weekly* 4. *Library Journal*

1.2.6 The Future: Graphic Novels and Tomorrow

Comic art continues to grow and to evolve. Artists, such as the ever-innovative Scott McCloud, are slowly trading in their ink for electrons as they create story images on the Web. In the virtually limitless canvas of cyberspace, artists are reinventing style and form, quite often shattering the concept of the "page."

The artists in the late eighteenth century first melded words, pictures, shifting points of view, and multiple characters and invented comic strips. The comic artists of the 1940s expanded panels into pages and made comic books. Creative writers in the 1970s and 1980s breathed life into comic books and brought forth original graphic novels.

Innovative artists thus for this century have stretched stories, color, composition, and form to the Internet, creating digital graphic novels. Online comic art has no "gravity"—the art can go up, down, backwards, and sideways, something unique to the electronic medium! This comic art cannot be easily printed on paper and enjoyed in the same fashion. To perhaps criminally paraphrase a recent movie, consider that "You must only try to realize the its not the book that is moving, it is you . . . there is no book."

However, as librarians deeply understand, sometimes the most attractive of stories are the ones you can open, touch, and imagine—exploring the mental worlds that exist only within the pages of a very real, very tangible book. There has never been a "convert" to a new story who, upon finishing the last glorious phrases of some newly discovered electronic fiction, has ever tried to reach out and hug a Web page.

1.2.7 Summary

- Comic art has been used to express ideas for millennia.
- Comic art has achieved popularity, acclaim, and credibility in the twentieth Century.
- Artists around the world have provided a rich and diverse history of comic art.
- Comic art is extending to the World Wide Web.
- Many industry journals are available to assist librarians with developing collections of graphic novels.

1.3 GENRES

Just like any library collection, graphic novels tell a wide variety of stories, from nonfiction and informational books to different types of fiction. A graphic novel can be found that can fit into most any YA or children's area.

1.3.1 Types of Graphic Novels

Graphic novels and comic art are used to tell a wide variety of stories. Like any type of fictional story, GNs can be separated into distinct genres. The first distinction within graphic novels is the one encountered when examining any other format: Is the material fiction or nonfiction? After this distinction is made, subsequent separation follows logically, and along traditional lines.

1.3.2 Nonfiction Topics

While fiction works embody the majority of the graphic novel market, there also exist nonfiction works on diverse subjects, including biography, history, and science. Currently, there are not enough subjects represented in a comic art format to justify special classification, however some "not entirely fiction" stories do deserve special mention, as these lists indicate.

BIOGRAPHY

One important nonfiction topic presented through comic art is that of biography. Some storytellers choose to relay their story visually because it can bring an intimacy between the reader and the central characters.

Pedro and Me: Friendship, Loss, and What I Learned, by Judd Winick.
Maus: A Survivor's Tale, by Art Spiegelman.
The Amazing True Story of a Teenage Single Mom, by K. Arnoldi.

HISTORY

Historical information and dramatizations are also conveyed through comic art. As with biographies, graphic novels show history in a fresh light, free from dry text and aging photographs. This always-fresh look is more appealing to young adults.

Fallout: J. Robert Oppenheimer, Leo Szilard, and the Political Science of the Atomic Bomb, by Jim Ottaviani.
Fax from Sarajevo, by Joe Kubert.
Palestine, by Joe Sacco.

SCIENCE

Dignifying Science and *Two-Fisted Science*, by Jim Ottaviani.
Clan Apis, by Jay Hosler.

ART

Two notable titles exist that are self-referential in that they are about comic art. Scott McCloud uses comic art to discuss the theory, mechanics, and psychology involved in creating successful comics.

Understanding Comics and *Reinventing Comics,* by Scott McCloud.

1.3.3 Fiction Genres

Graphic novels most commonly convey fictional stories and can be broken down into the same categories that libraries have used for decades. Drama, science fiction and fantasy, horror, western, and general fiction are popular genre designations. However, in the genres of romance, mystery, and western, there are not many titles available. While there are titles published in these genres, there are too few to justify giving them a separate classification. Perhaps, as the market changes, there will be more titles available. In the meantime, however, it is best to classify them as general fiction.

The two categories of fiction most often associated with graphic novels are *superheroes* and *Manga*. These categories contain sufficient titles to warrant being considered separate classifications of graphic novel fiction.

- **Superheroes.** This is the classic superpowerful hero against the evil powerful villain that has been so successful in the comic book industry for years. Superheroes that started in comic books are now being featured in full-length graphic novels. While many literary characters have heroic qualities, comics and graphic novels have elevated the classic hero to superhero status. This exaggerated characterization, combined with fantastic locales, found fertile ground in the images of early comic art and established the superhero as a distinct genre of comic art storytelling.
- **Manga.** While actually a style of Japanese comic art, Manga has a very dedicated following among American youth. Because this foreign style is so popular, it is often convenient for libraries to consider it as a separate genre, despite the fact that any genre of story can be illustrated in this art style. Patrons who enjoy Manga do not often differentiate between science fiction Manga, romance Manga, and so forth. For most teens, Manga is Manga. If it is shelved together, they will find it.

Popular Fiction Genres of Graphic Novels
• Superhero
• Fantasy
• Science Fiction
• Manga

DRAMA/REAL LIFE

This genre is one in which graphic novels excel. Many original stories are produced exclusively in this format. While a fine line away from being general fiction, some teen readers are drawn to stories about overcoming life's troubles. Readers of Lurlene McDaniels, for example, might enjoy Talbot's *The Tale of One Bad Rat,* a very good story about an abused teenager coming into her own.

Road to Perdition, by Max Allan Collins.
The Tale of One Bad Rat, by Bryan Talbot.
Ghost World, by Daniel Clowes.

SCIENCE FICTION

Science fiction would seem to lend itself readily to stories in comic art. Unfortunately, science fiction graphic novels find themselves frequently overshadowed by other media, such as film, television, and even role playing games. *Star Wars* and *Star Trek* have many stories told in the graphic novel format. As graphic novels increase in popularity, there might be more movies and television shows that come from science fiction GNs, rather than having the videos inspire a plethora of comics. And if Manga were not classified as a separate genre, many Manga titles would be classified as science fiction.

FANTASY

Typically dominated by the superheroes subcategory, well-illustrated graphic novels are a perfect showcase for both classic and original tales of the fantastic. Fantastic themes are also common in the Japanese Manga style of comic art.

City of Light, City of Dark, by Avi.
The Books of Magic, by Neil Gaiman.
Castle Waiting, by Linda Medley.

HORROR

Comic art is used to tell stories ranging from gothic to the otherworldly. Many titles are available in this genre, although materials should be previewed with care. Some excellent material, such as Alan Moore's *From Hell,* may be beneficial in an adult collection, but it is definitely not appropriate for all teens or children.

Sandman (series), by Neil Gaiman.
Preacher (series), by Garth Ennis.

CLASSICS

Many literary works have been adapted into graphic novels. Publication of such "illustrated classics" has been somewhat sporadic. If desired titles are out of print, keep checking. Many classic works of American and English literature have been adapted, of which a few are *The Scarlet Letter, Moby Dick,* and *Hamlet.*

Little Lit (series), edited by Art Spiegelman.
The Illiad and The Odyssey, adapted by Marcia Williams.
Moby Dick and *The Princess and the Frog,* adapted by Will Eisner.

GENERAL FICTION

As with a text-based fiction or paperback collection, the term *general* is a catchall for material that is not otherwise easily categorized. It can include humor, satire, comedy, or any genre of material that may not be copious (or popular) enough to merit a unique classification.

High Society (*Cerberus, Volume 2*), by Dave Sim.
A Contract with God, by Will Eisner.
Age of Reptiles, by Ricardo Delgado.
Bone (series), by Jeff Smith.

SUPERHEROES

Superheroes are perhaps the most popular and obvious genre of comics and graphic novels. A subgenre that crosses fantasy and adventure, these tales of superhumans have been the predominant form of comic storytelling since the early part of the twentieth century. The superhero genre has become inexorably linked with the phrase "comic books." Major publishers of superhero comics are DC Comics and Marvel Comics, each publishing dozens of titles monthly.

Batman: The Dark Knight Returns, by Frank Miller.
Marvels, by Kurt Busiek.
Kingdom Come, by Mark Waid.
Kurt Busiek's Astro City (series), by Kurt Busiek.

MANGA

Manga is, quite simply, Japanese comics. This distinct artistic style has become very popular with people around the globe. There are several things that separate this style from Western/American comics.

- Character's possess exaggerated physical features.
- Motion takes place subjectively, rather than objectively.
- The story relies heavily on visual cues rather than text.

Some believe that the simplified, very expressive features of a character in Manga allow the reader to identify easily with that character. Large eyes, stylized hair, and exaggerated mouths are often drawn with simple line art. This exaggeration and simplicity, some believe, allows the viewer to place him- or herself in the story.

Motion in Manga comic art takes place from the character's point of view. The world blurs as the character moves, much as what one would see in real life. American comics, on the other hand, show the background scenery as static, with the character moving, trailed by motion lines. The subjective aspect of motion in Manga also contributes to a viewer's ability to place him- or herself within the story. For an example of this, see the illustration Motion in American and Japanese Comics (p. 32).

Most storylines in Manga, particularly in the action genres, rely heavily on visual images rather than textual cues. This may seem obvious since action scenes typically do not have extensive dialogue and they contain many panels of movement. But Manga's action stories, in general, typically use less text than American action/superhero comics. Character relationships, mood, tone, and other elements of storytelling are expressed visually rather than through narrative or exposition. This focus on visualizing the story allows the viewer to flow from one panel to the next, increasing his or her sense of immersion in the story.

Many Manga are based on *anime*—animated films and television shows. "Japanimation" has been increasing in popularity since the 1960s. Children and teens today are accustomed to viewing this style of animation on television and in videos. They will easily make the transition to reading graphic novels that highlight their favorite characters.

Manga is an artistic style, not a distinct genre. It contains stories from all genres, for all ages of readers. In Japan, comics are not only for children; this art style is used to produce comic art for every conceivable age, occupation, interest, and vice. The style also extends into comic strips and animated movies.

Considering Manga as a separate genre is an oversimplification, akin to classifying all American comics into a single genre. However, many American readers of Manga are avid (bordering on the fanatical) collectors and will seek out more of the same. Inversely, readers who do not like the style will generally not read a graphic novel in the Manga style regardless of its theme. Labeling and shelving Manga in a consistent fashion will help dedicated readers find them.

Another reason to separate Manga as a unique genre is that it is not often written for children. With the exception of fad titles, such as *Pokemon* or *Digimon,* most Manga titles are for teenagers and adults. Manga stories often contain cultural references or situations that, while perfectly acceptable in Japanese society, may not be appropriate for a reader of the same age elsewhere. For example, the *Ranma* $\frac{1}{2}$ is a series about a teenage boy who falls into a cursed spring. Thereafter, his gender magically changes when he is touched by either warm or cold water. This can lead to humorous situations, particularly when romantic interests begin occurring. This is where cultural mores come into play. It is acceptable in Japan to portray some nudity in comics. For example, in the case of poor Ranma, if he is showering and a friend plays a practical joke on him by changing the temperature of the water, the reader will see a panel or two of Ranma's nude feminine form from the waist up. While contextual and cultural, these incidental images are generally not considered appropriate for all children in America.

Some Japanese Manga, however, does not give away its content through its title. This is mainly because of the translation from Japanese to English. If a title's literal translation in English is not considered marketable, some license will be taken. It is highly recommended to focus on reviews and recommendations when obtaining Manga. Rumiko Takahashi has written prodigiously, and some of her popular series are *Ranma ½, Maison Ikkoku,* and *Inu-Yasha.* Hayao Miyazaki is another popular Japanese artist. Creator of the *Nausicaa of the Valley of Wind* series, his work has also received acclaim through the movie *Spirited Away.* Other popular Manga stories are *Fushigi Yugi* by Yu Watase, *Gon* by Masashi Tanaka, and *Adolf* by Osama Tezuka.

1.3.4 Summary

- Graphic novels are a unique form of storytelling.
- Graphic novels can include fiction and nonfiction.
- Graphic novels can cover many genres of fiction and many categories of nonfiction.

2

Graphic Novels in Libraries

2.1 Collection Development

    2.1.1 Collection Development

    2.1.2 The Five Cs of Graphic Novel Librarianship

    2.1.3 Making the Case

    2.1.4 Summary

2.2 Acquisition

    2.2.1 Acquisition

    2.2.2 Local Sources: Shops and Chains

    2.2.3 Shipping Sources: Distributors and Jobbers

    2.2.4 Summary

2.3 Cataloging

    2.3.1 Approaches to Cataloging

    2.3.2 Approaches to Age Levels

    2.3.3 A Cataloger's Guide to Comic Art

    2.3.4 Summary

2.4 Collection Maintenance and Defense

    2.4.1 Maintenance

    2.4.2 The Danger of Crime

    2.4.3 The Danger of Wear

    2.4.4 The Danger of Challenges

    2.4.5 Determine the Value of a Collection: Statistics

    2.4.6 Growing Pains: Weeding and Relocation

    2.4.7 Summary

2.1 COLLECTION DEVELOPMENT

Not every graphic novel is created equally. Careful selection criteria should be followed, as with the selection of any library material. Determining a need for a GN collection, responding to a patron's desires, and previewing selections can provide some focus to the collection development process.

2.1.1 Collection Development

Collection development is the process of responsibly selecting appropriate material for the library and the community. What types of materials can be put in a collection of graphic novels? A general rule of thumb for stocking a graphic novel collection is to include any "thick" comic book in that area. This would include a bound collection of comic books but it would exclude a compilation of comic strips. Patrons who are interested in true GNs are often attracted to the bound collections. Comic strip compilations, however, will not always appeal to the reader of graphic novels. This rough advice works fine on a small scale. To build a robust and supported collection, though, it must have a focus and administrative backing.

Administrators of public and school libraries have a very broad view of library organization. These people focus on where the organization is and where it is moving. They balance the wishes of the community and the needs of the staff against the library's budgets, policies, and image.

To gain support for including graphic novels in the collection, and to help potential supporters understand the benefits of this type of collection, several things should be considered.

- **Why do we need graphic novels in the library?** How does our library benefit? Will graphic novels be considered a credible investment for us?
- **Will the materials be used?** Which materials will circulate at our library? With our patrons?
- **Do graphic novels fit into our library's mission and goals?** Do our patrons want comic art materials? Can we commit to this type of collection?
- **How do we select appropriate material for our youth, teen, and adult patrons?** What is needed for a strong collection? How does this collection affect our collection development policy?
- **How much of a budget will this collection need?** What are the costs? What is the price range for different types of books?

A useful tool to use when answering these questions is the "Five Cs of Graphic Novel Librarianship." These help collection developers view their specialized collection from an administrative perspective. Following these tips will do more than create a packet of information to guide collection growth; it can help librarians who are starting new collections organize a proposal to help gain the support of both library administrators and staff.

2.1.2 The Five Cs of Graphic Novel Librarianship

Many factors must be considered while working with public funds in general, as well as when expanding library collections and services to young adults. Five of these in particular are credibility, circulation, commitment, collection, and cost.

The Five Cs of Graphic Novel Librarianship
Credibility
Circulation
Commitment
Collection
Cost

Not all organizations have a standing line item in their budgets for graphic novels and public and school libraries in general are not given unlimited budgets with which to purchase materials. The Five Cs can help guide the growth of an existing graphic novel collection, and they can justify the creation of a new collection. If they are considered while developing a graphic novel collection, you will be an informed purchaser as well as be able to defend a title's place in the collection.

THE FIRST C: CREDIBILITY

Throughout their long history, comics—and now, graphic novels—were considered kid's stuff, at best. At their worst moment, comic art was seen as a disruptive social influence that created hooligans and delinquents. This misconception may still hold in the minds of some librarians and educators; this is the stigma than many people still subscribe to, and it raises the question, Why have comics in a library?

How can comics be seen in a new, more positive light? Consider these observations:

- **Graphic novels inspire art and imagination.** They inspire a reader's active participation to bring the characters to life. Many young people take an interest in art, and they often express their own stories through comic art.
- **Graphic novels improve visual literacy.** Children and teens are a visual generation. They are growing up with television, computers, and video

games. They spend most of their time processing images and sounds rather than reading words. Our electronic age requires its citizens to process information visually. Comics provide a platform that shows words and images in a mutually reinforcing framework, one that promotes visual literacy. This can help students process information "beyond the words," one key to stimulating visual literacy.

- **Graphic novels and comic art are attractive to children and teens for recreational reading.** Today's youth show a preference for comic art material. In 1999, a Newspaper Association of America report noted that 43 percent of American teenagers read the newspaper comic sections, more than the number of teens who look at the front page. Simmons, a marketing research company, published a study in 2000 reporting that comic books are the favorite reading material of 41 percent of children age six to eleven.

- **Graphic novels increase library traffic.** A comic or graphic novel collection can attract new readers of *all ages*. Some libraries report as much as an 80 percent increase in patronage to their young adult area.

- **Graphic novels increase circulation of noncomic books.** Many graphic novels have tie-ins to books and, more recently, movies. Some libraries have reported 25 percent increases in overall collection circulation after adding graphic novels to their collections. A few have even noted that their few shelves of graphic novels circulate as much as a dozen shelves of young adult fiction.

- **Graphic novels attract reluctant readers.** Illustrations work with the text to provide contextual reinforcement as the story progresses. This maintains the interest of challenged readers in a nonthreatening manner as they build reading confidence.

- **Graphic novels promote literacy.** Many educators feel that reading anything will build literacy skills. Full-length graphic novels contain, on average, 168 pages and 12,400 words, while some reach as high as 20,000 words. Juvenile fiction novels can top 30,000 words, but reluctant readers can make it up in volume with graphic novels—teens often read multiple graphic novels, devouring thousands of words without realizing it. This is a very useful literacy tool for reluctant readers who ordinarily would not read a "regular" book. In many cases, literacy is such a high priority for public and school libraries that they are willing to try almost anything to help challenged or reluctant readers develop a love of reading.

- **Graphic novels help develop language skills.** In comic art, the images support the text. This is helpful for ESOL (English for Speakers of Other Languages) students. The reader receives visual assistance in understanding the text. The inverse is also true—English-speaking students studying other languages can benefit from foreign editions of graphic novels in French, German, Spanish, Russian, Japanese, and other languages.

- **Graphic novels are used by public and school libraries.** Many libraries and schools around the world are taking an interest in comic art and graphic novels. These popular books are used in classrooms and for library programs and are a dynamic part of library collections.

Why are they so popular? First, they are easy to read and comprehend. The visual images tell part of the story, lessening the burden on the reader. Second, comics often tell fun, exciting stories that draw the reader into the action. They are also quick to read—a graphic novel can be enjoyed in much less time than can a novel or even a short story.

An often overlooked reason why comics are popular is that it is rare to find a child who is *required* to read one. When children choose graphic novels, they sit down to read them because it is *their* idea. There is no pressure of being graded. It is not to *learn* something. It is just for fun! (The fun part, for the adults, comes when a teacher actually assigns a student to read a graphic novel. Most teens are excited to learn their teacher is actually *cool!*)

Why Are Graphic Novels Popular?

- They are easy to read.
- They are easy to understand.
- They contain fun and exciting stories.
- They are quick to read.

Scott McCloud, the comics theorist, has his own views on why comics are so popular. He refers to the phenomenon as "reader engagement" and cites many popular Manga stories. What contributes to reader engagement in Manga? Two important elements are their simple features and their first-person point of view.

Simple features. As character artwork becomes less complex, the features become less distinct. The result is a face with as few lines as possible. This is something at which Manga artists excel. McCloud feels this simplicity of character allows the reader to place himself in the story, to see herself in the character. This is because a person's internal self-view consists of the awareness of mouth and eye position and facial tension, and not so much on the actual features of their own face. Therefore, we are able to see ourselves in comic characters rendered in a minimalist way.

First-person point of view. In Japanese comics, the backgrounds are usually more detailed than the characters, and motion lines are drawn in a unique fashion. This reinforces the identification the reader experiences with the character. The character is minimalist; the backgrounds are more detailed and lifelike.

Consider the illustration Motion in American and Japanese Comics, in which Smiley explores motion lines. In American (and European) comics style, motion lines are drawn trailing behind the moving object, in this case Smiley. The background remains still and only the character is in motion. This is how a scene would be perceived by an outside viewer.

In Japanese comics, however, Smiley is seen as static while the background moves past him. Observe how the moon and the trees in the example have motion lines trailing behind them. This is how motion would be perceived from a firsthand perspective—the world moves past you as you run. This is one of the key elements of Japanese Manga and one reason why it is so popular with a video generation of young adults. Manga lets the reader share in the world of the characters.

Smiley in the Forest of the Night

Motion in American and Japanese Comics.

Comic art uses these techniques to help readers "insert" themselves into the story. They owe their popularity to this psychological phenomenon. Because of their popularity, and their virtually universal ease of comprehension, they are appropriate for public and school libraries. In meeting the recreational reading needs of teens, their presence in a library's collection will entice young adults to visit the library.

THE SECOND C: CIRCULATION

Service affects statistics. Many libraries count everything—the number of copies made at the public copier, the number of people who walk through the doors, and how many students are spoken to at an outreach book talk. Statistics are the lifeblood of nonprofit agencies because in the absence of monetary income, these numbers measure community service. One of the most important statistics is that of collection circulation: how many items have been loaned to the patrons.

Circulation statistics also justify the need for—or the expansion of—a graphic novel collection. Tracking the circulation of a GN collection is greatly facilitated if your library uses an automation system and has a separate collection designation for these items. Regular statistical reports will show how many items are being borrowed (**2.4: Collection Maintenance and Defense** will discuss how to use the statistics to determine the health of your collection).

Pilot Collections

It is possible to obtain statistics about graphic novel circulation even when separate statistical designations are unavailable. Most libraries have graphic novels, having collected a few randomly (or accidentally) over the years. Even if there is no separate location or statistical category for them, they can still be used to test circulation. Creating a pilot collection is one way to test the waters without investing a great deal of money. It can be time intensive, but the results will provide solid evidence about the viability of a graphic novel collection.

A pilot collection is a special display of items that are monitored over a period of months to determine popularity. Use statistics are gathered before and after the display period. This display will introduce patrons to the potential collection, and it will provide hard data that can help justify the need for a dedicated collection later on.

Benefits of a Pilot Collection
Educates patrons about graphic novels.
Provides statistical data about circulation.
Provides an opportunity to freshen the collection.

To create a pilot collection, pull together any existing materials on the shelves that are in a comic format. This includes comic strips, comic books, bound collections, and graphic novels. In this temporary collection, thematic cohesion is maintained by each item being part of the comic art family. Consider purchasing a few titles from the Core Titles listing in the back of this book. New items will freshen the display and make it more attractive.

How to Create a Pilot Collection

- Gather all comic-format material in one place.
- Prepare a Pilot Collection Worksheet to help track each item.
- Display the material in a prominent location.
- Determine new use counts.
- Calculate the changes.

Track each item's use over a few months. This will allow an apples-to-apples comparison of which types of comic art are most popular. Since comic strip compilations are on display with graphic novels in the same place during the same period, you will be able to accurately compare their use on equal terms. Create a Pilot Collection Worksheet that is an inventory of the items on display; include the author, title, genre, type of comic art, the date it was added to the collection, and its circulation up to this point. It is helpful to add a column for the item's age, in months. Dividing the use by the age gives an average circulation-per-month (predisplay).

Display the material in a prominent location for a few months. Promote it with signs. Make bookmarks that list the titles. Verbally "up sell" the items during checkout transactions. As the items return from circulation, reshelve them with the pilot collection. Watch to see which patrons browse the collection spontaneously.

When the survey period is over, pull the collection from the shelves and write down the new use counts on your worksheet. Subtract the previous use from the current use to determine how many times each item was checked out during the display period.

When the study is over review the worksheet. Which genres experienced the greatest increase? Which types of comic art were utilized the most? Which titles had the most circulation? The answers to these questions will illustrate how the patrons responded to comic art and to graphic novels.

This study may appear to be time consuming, and it may be difficult for any staff member to find the time to do it. Tracking a pilot collection would be a perfect opportunity, though, for a member of the library's teen group or for a volunteer to learn more about how (and why) libraries work. Enlist some help, distribute the work, and try it!

What Belongs in a Graphic Novel Collection?
• Original graphic novels. • Bound collections of comic art from comic books and magazines.
What Does Not Belong in a Graphic Novel Collection **(But Would Work Well in a Pilot Collection)?**
• Books on how to draw comics, unless done exclusively in comic art. • Books on the history of comic books, such as works discussing the evolution of the *Batman* or *Superman* characters, unless done exclusively in comic art. • Collections of comic strips, such as *Dilbert* or *Garfield*. • Single-issue comic books. • Art History, unless done exclusively in comic art. • Anything not done *exclusively* in comic art.

THE THIRD C: COMMITMENT

Methods of collecting graphic novels in a library can range from the ad hoc "buy and shelve it" to a more complex process that includes updating collection development policies and modifying cataloging procedures.

Commitment to building a successful graphic novel collection must come from many levels of the library—from administration and from staff. One useful method for gaining administrative support is to consider that a collection of graphic novels can support the existing goals and needs of the library. This is done by considering the library's mission statement and its collection development policy and through soliciting feedback from patrons.

A graphic novel collection can be used to implement several aspects of a mission statement. Make associations between policies and the issues discussed in **Credibility** at the beginning of this chapter. Consider the following questions:

- **Is recreational reading a component?** From the perspective of a teen library patron, comics can be fun. This means that graphic novels have a high value for recreational reading.
- **Is reading or literacy mentioned?** From an educator's point of view, continued exposure to reading materials can build literacy skills.
- **Is community service to your school or town an important goal of the library?** Popular collections can increase patronage and circulation; it brings people in the door so you can put a book in their hands.

When working with any new collection, it is advisable to review the library's collection development policy. This statement is what guides the materials selection process and helps library staff create a useful, well-balanced collection. Look at the collection development policy, and consider:

- **Should additions to the library support educational curricula?** While graphic novels are an excellent way to encourage recreational reading, they also have several educational uses. See **3.3: Education** for more information on how GNs can be used in educational environments.
- **Should they complement other library holdings?** Graphic novels are an "in-between" medium. Media tie-ins abound with comics—movies are based on GNs, some GNs are adapted from books, GNs have even been based on, of all things, video games. Graphic novels can both complement the cultural habitat of young adults and help create a bridge to more traditional library holdings.
- **Should we acquire both current and older materials?** This is where the goals of the collection are focused. Is there a need to collect all graphic novels, the old and the new? Do existing holdings need to be expanded by these popular comic novels? Will they be collected in a scholarly fashion, or will their purpose be to attract teens to the library?
- **Should we order books and periodicals to support the library collections?** Consider purchases of books about drawing art and magazines about collecting comics to supplement a new graphic novel collection. For example, if the library has a video collection, are there complementary books of movie reviews in the collection? Does the fiction area receive high use? Is there a copy of *Genreflecting* or other readers' advisory tools available? The collection development policy may give latitude to support and extend the use of a graphic novel collection, whether new or already established.
- **Should gifts or donations be accepted?** It is possible for patrons and local businesses to support a graphic novel collection through donations. Does this policy offer guidelines to help evaluate these types of materials? (It is possible to receive rather substantial donations, so consider beforehand how many would be *too* many.)

An important step to justifying a graphic novel collection is to demonstrate how it would meet a need. The easiest way to learn this is to ask the patrons what they think. Often, casual remarks from teen and adult patrons about comics and graphic novels can help identify not only what items are needed in the collection, but also how they choose to spend their reading time.

Libraries without a graphic novel collection are advised to run a temporary, or pilot, collection before surveying patrons. The pilot collection educates patrons about graphic novels and what can be found in collections of them. Surveys refine the goals and expectations about a collection. Patron feedback is invaluable when planning the directions in which this unique collection will grow. Educate the patrons and then determine what they want.

Libraries that have an established GN collection may find it helpful to perform an occasional survey. This will help staff and developers stay informed of the patrons' interests. It can help determine if the selection process and book displays are working well, and it will point out how the collection is viewed. It is also a good way to get ideas on how to extend services to young adults by directly asking, "Do you want GN-related programs and events?" and "Are you interested in contests about comic art?"

When adding or expanding a graphic novel collection, some libraries survey their patrons at the beginning of the project. While surveys provide excellent feedback, they may not be the best tool to use at the beginning. Several librarians have faltered in their development of a collection by *asking* before *showing*. It was discovered that many patrons, including teens, are not even aware of what graphic novels are.

Well-meaning librarians have spent weeks informally talking to their young adult patrons, inquiring about their interest in comic books and graphic novels. "Graphic *what*?" was the common response. After displaying a pilot collection, however, the reaction was quite different: "These are cool! Get more!"

Another librarian asked her teen group if they liked graphic novels. This query was met with confused looks and negative remarks. A few weeks later, she overheard the young adults talking about some Manga titles they had found at a local bookstore and about their associated television series. This librarian looked over and said, "Guys, you're talking about graphic novels!" The surprised group responded, "*Those* are graphic novels? Great! Get some!"

Here are some suggestions to consider when discussing graphic novels and comics with patrons. Do not start out by explaining how graphic novels are different from comic books. Do not ask hypothetical questions. Instead, show the patrons what you have in mind. Give them a chance to browse the collection freely. Spend time casually soliciting opinions. Then, after the patrons have been exposed, run a formal survey. The responses at this time will be more accurate and the results more lasting. This is patron education at its best:

- Display materials.
- Discuss reactions.
- Determine preferences.

The pilot collection should adequately display the materials. It is also useful for obtaining an initial set of statistics to further justify a new collection. Casually talking about the comics with teens will elicit specific comments.

These can be documented and used to support a decision to add or to expand a graphic novel collection. A survey will give the teens a voice in how they want their library to grow.

Survey forms, such as the one below, can be used to ask specific questions. Surveying does not have to involve sitting down with a patron and peppering him or her with questions, although that is certainly one way to find out a teen's opinions. How can you distribute surveys?

- Leave surveys near the pilot collection to solicit spontaneous comments.
- Hand them to any patron who borrows (or returns) a graphic novel.
- Create a link on your library's Web page to a survey form.
- Use a local newspaper or ask for an outside sponsorship from your friends or teen groups. Local literary clubs might help too.
- Distribute them to English, reading, and art classes in junior and high schools.
- Discuss them in your teen advisory group meetings.

Try to blend several methods of distributing the survey form to ensure its exposure to a wide range of patrons who may be interested. If the responses are not as numerous as you had hoped for, offer a small incentive for teens to complete a survey. For example, pull one entry in a random drawing to win a prize, or buy a bag of bulk candy and give a piece to anyone who fills out a survey. (That is one rule of young adult service: Most teens will work for food.)

Surveys have one extra benefit—they can also be a form of promotion! Participating in a survey can give patrons an inside track on things that could be changing in their library. The sample survey form gives an example of how to learn what forms of comic art are desired by the patrons.

"Comics in the Library" Patron Survey Form

Comics in the Library!

Your library is considering expanding a collection of comics and graphic novels. Please take a moment to fill out this survey to let us know what you think!

1. **What types of fiction books do you enjoy reading? (circle as many as apply)**

General Fiction	True Stories	Science Fiction
Fantasy	Humor	Christian Fiction
Horror	Mystery	Other: _____
Romance	Westerns	

2. Do you enjoy reading comic books? Yes No
Would you borrow comic books from the library? Yes No
Which comic book(s) would you like to see in the library?

3. Do you enjoy reading books of comic strips, such as *Dilbert*, *Garfield*, etc.? Yes No
Should the library get more? Yes No
Which comic strip characters do you like the most? _____

4. Do you enjoy reading graphic novels (book-length comics)? Yes No
Should the library get more?
What titles or types of stories should we purchase?

5. Do you have any comments about the library having comic/ graphic novel material for you to borrow?

6. Have you ever seen a movie based on a graphic novel? Yes No
Have you ever read a book based on a graphic novel? Yes No

7. Demographics.
Gender: Male Female
Age: 5–8 9–12 13–15 16–18 19+
Grade: _____

Compile the survey results and then evaluate them. Which age range provided the most responses? Is there a demand for more comic strip collections? Do the patrons want comic books or graphic novels? Review the comments for any unique quotes, either for or against comics and graphic novels.

THE FOURTH C: COLLECTION

A pilot collection demonstrates how a graphic novel collection would be used and it generates useful statistics. The patron survey provides feedback and, hopefully, suggestions and recommendations. Now the question is, What to purchase? Answer this by compiling a graphic novel wish list. Be ready to jot down the specific titles of comic books, graphic novels, comic strip compilations, and any favorite genres that were mentioned. The first step is to list titles and genres that could work in your library.

- **Review the patron surveys** for recommended titles and genres. The most advisable way to start or expand a GN collection is to begin with what the teens want. Add these titles to the list.

- **Refer to your Pilot Collection Worksheet** and locate the items (or genres) with the greatest improvement in "circs-per-month." Add these to the wish list.
- **Pick some recommended titles** from Chapter 4 of this book, "Core Titles Listing," and add them to the wish list.
- **Check vendor catalogs** or order a catalog from Diamond Comics Distributors (bookshelf.diamondcomics.com). This is perhaps the best way to obtain pricing and availability information.

After making your wish list, there is now a basic plan for what to purchase. However, how do you determine which are the best choices?

Purchasing Made Easy! A GN Wish List

- Solicit patron recommendations.
- Note popular genres and titles.
- Obtain catalogs that offer graphic novels.
- See it for yourself.

As with other books, many organizations and librarians review graphic novels. There are many excellent review sources in professional journals and online at Web sites and discussion groups. Using these sources will not only help justify the titles on the wish list, they will also make recommendations for future purchases and provide the current "best-of-the-best" list.

Recommended Journals for GN Reviews

Voice of Youth Advocates
School Library Journal
Publisher's Weekly
Library Journal

Recommended Web Sites and E-mail Discussion Lists for GN Reviews

Diamond Comics (bookshelf.diamondcomics.com)
Comics Get Serious: Graphic Novel Reviews (www.rationalmagic.com/
   Comics/Comics.html)
GNLIB-L on the Web: Graphic Novels in Libraries e-mail list support Web
   site (www.angelfire.com/comics/gnlib)
The Comics Journal (www.tcj.com)

Recommended Magazines for Comic and GN News
Previews (http://previews.diamondcomics.com) *Comic Shop News*, often available free at comic book stores. *Wizard Magazine* *Comics Buyers Guide*

In addition to reviews, the comics industry regularly recognizes leading artists (and titles) with awards. The Eisner and the Harvey are two prominent awards named after artists in the industry. They indicate the best of the best from the industry's point of view. Be aware, however, that not every title that receives an award is appropriate for public or school libraries. More information about comic book awards can be found at the Comic Book Award Archive (http://users.rcn.com/aardy/comics/awards/). This site also mentions several non-American comics awards from the United Kingdom, France, Sweden, and Germany. For more information on the Harvey Award, visit www.harveyawards.com.

Journal reviews and awards are quick ways to assess the value of a title, but actually reading a graphic novel is one of the best ways to determine its appropriateness for your particular GN collection. Graphic novels use artwork to tell a story, and this art can vary greatly in style and content. Not every reviewer focuses on the artistic content of the GN he or she discusses. What may work in one library may not be acceptable in another.

While learning the ropes of working with graphic novels, it is very helpful to physically touch a copy of each title before purchasing it. Look through your Wish List and pick a few titles to inter-library loan for review. Visit a comic book store and ask to flip through a copy, or simply purchase it outright for a personal collection. For those people who are inexperienced with graphic novels, reading a few graphic novels will give you a first-hand perspective on what they are, and why they could be popular.

What do you look for in a good graphic novel? While you flip through a graphic novel, ask yourself some questions.

- **How many pages does it have?** Does it completely tell the story?
- **Is the artwork clear?** Does it support the story? Is there any nudity or violence?
- **Is the text readable?** What age or reading level is the vocabulary? Does it contain strong language or epithets? If so, is it integral to the story? Is it contextual or cultural?
- **Are the pages understandable?** Do the panels flow in an easily understood manner? Do the text and artwork complement each other?

- **Is it a good story?** What would be an appropriate age level for this title? Are there mature themes? Which library audience would be most likely to enjoy it—children, teens, or adults?
- **Consider the audience,** the community, and the collection development objectives.
- **Is it durable** enough to withstand dozens of loans?
- **Is it trendy** or dated in such a way that its use will decrease after a short time?
- **Is anything in it potentially objectionable?** Is it likely to be open to challenges?

These guidelines will rule out poor artwork and story as well as filter out titles that could cause a variety of problems later on. When the opportunity arises to read a GN prior to purchase, remember these suggestions.

THE FIFTH C: COST

After evaluating some titles on your wish list, it's time to look at the bottom line: How much will all this cost? An initial budget must be created.

For each item on the list, write down the retail price. Consult catalogs, comic book stores, and online retail sites. Calculate the total cost, as if this were a single order. Now comes the big question: Can the order for that amount of graphic novels be approved? If so, then start placing an order!

Quite often, one cannot buy everything at one time. Narrowing the focus can help prioritize which items can be ordered now and which can wait until later. Prioritized ordering is one way to reduce costs and to spread the risk over time. Risk, in this context, means investing in items that may not circulate as well as expected. By ordering these potentially "low-circ" titles sparingly, the collection can focus on high traffic items. One method of prioritizing is to consider each item as a "must have," a "wanna get," or a "should purchase" selection. This practice is designed to maximize circulation while minimizing cost. It focuses on getting the most bang for the buck out of a graphic novel collection.

- **Must have.** Titles in this category are patron recommendations and very popular genres. Graphic novel series, particularly Manga series, are often in this category.
- **Wanna get.** These are books needed to round out the collection, or to expand into another genre.
- **Should purchase.** In this category full materials that generally supplement the collection, such as material on drawing comic art for the nonfiction collection, or those graphic novel titles that are well respected but may not be borrowed much. (Surprisingly, literary classics adapted to

comic art circulate better than one might expect. Do not automatically relegate them to a tertiary purchase level.)

These three categories will cover most graphic novel titles. Series, though, can quickly deplete a budget, particularly if they are being ordered in a single set. Most GN series, particularly Manga, can span more than twenty books. As with any series of books, however, series of graphic novels are very popular. To maximize patron interest, and to minimize expenses, develop a series a few titles at a time, preferably in sequential order. Even if an entire series can be purchased at once, consider ordering only a few titles at a time. This allows time to observe patron interest. If the titles from the series are rarely on the shelf, then it is safe to order the next batch. Letting new series titles trickle in also prolongs the excitement of getting in new books. Maintain interest. Draw it out. Order regularly. Remember, though—teens grow up. Make sure the series is completely acquired within a reasonable period of time to maintain the interest of interested teens, as younger teens begin to explore your GN collection.

For larger libraries, another method of reducing costs is to spread the collection across several branch locations. Rather than investing in a copy of each title for each location, "spread" ordering allows each location to receive new titles. Duplicates can then be purchased for only the most in-demand graphic novels.

Some librarians experienced with graphic novels advise others to be prepared for demand. After a few beginning purchases, there may be a need to consider ordering multiple copies if a title is anticipated to be in high demand.

Value-Added Paperbacks

Paperback graphic novels may not last as long as hardbacks, but teens are more apt to check them out if they can be stuffed into their backpacks or back pockets. There may be extra circulations in store if two paperback copies are purchased instead of a single hardback copy.

The average cost of a hardcover graphic novel is about $29.95. Some titles retail for as little as $25 while other bound collections can reach as high as $40. For paperbacks, the prices are more reasonable—$13.50 is the average. Some titles sell for $5 to $8, while others can go up to $20. A $100 investment can bring seven to twelve new graphic novels into your collection. Some libraries spend $500 per month on graphic novels; others spread that amount out over the course of a year.

The last cost involved in a graphic novel collection—furniture and shelving—depends on the amount of space your facility has available for it. Graphic novels are oversized compared to most young adult fiction. The width of a GN ranges from $6\frac{1}{2}$ inches to 9 inches, and the height can vary between 6 inches to 12 inches. These sizes will readily fit on standard adjustable shelving. Some graphic novels, however, can extend to over 14 inches in height or width. Just as with many nonfiction books, oversized GN titles exist. Consider if the space selected for the collection can accommodate these odd sizes. Many libraries adjust their existing shelving to match the collection, use spinner racks, or simply display the collection on top of shelving ranges. If additional equipment is needed—even down to extra bookends—check with equipment suppliers or library supply catalogs and incorporate these costs into the proposal.

2.1.3 Making the Case

This process has helped you compile information about a graphic novel collection. This information can be used to support the growth of an existing collection or to facilitate the creation of a new one. It is likely the data indicates that such a collection would be viable and can be complementary to the library's goals. This information can be organized into a proposal that can serve not only as a framework that defines a new collection, but also as a guide to educate library staff about graphic novels in general. Remember the "Five Cs of Graphic Novel Librarianship" when drafting this document. Use them as a framework for a growth plan or for a proposal to create a graphic novel collection. In each section, include the following information.

- **Credibility.** Explain how graphic novels can benefit libraries. Present ideas about how they can help inspire a student's desire to learn. Talk about how teens respond to visual media.
- **Circulation.** Explain how circulation statistics can be derived from a dedicated collection. Present an overview of the results of the pilot collection, mentioning specific changes and popular items or genres.
- **Commitment.** Explain how graphic novels support the library's mission statement and work with its collection development policy. Use data and comments from surveys to demonstrate how your library's patrons feel about comics and graphic novels.
- **Collection.** Present the final wish list of titles as a recommended initial order (or series of orders). Explain how they were determined by consulting reviews, policies, and first-hand assessments. Include supportive elements from the collection development policy.

- **Cost.** Present a draft budget for the collection's first few years. Explain how costs will be managed through prioritized ordering.

This basic format can answer the questions asked by co-workers and administrators.

2.1.4 Summary

- View a library's needs from an administrative perspective.
- Tie graphic novels into a library's collection development policy and mission statement.
- Gather statistics with a pilot collection.
- Survey patrons.
- Determine and recommend an initial budget.
- Review and select titles.
- Compile a proposal packet for a new collection.

2.2 ACQUISITION

Many traditional library vendors are distributing graphic novels as a component of their regular service to libraries. When used in conjunction with local stores or specialty comic book shops, an increasing variety of quality graphic novels are available for public and school libraries to choose from.

2.2.1 Acquisition

Acquisition is the first step to bringing new material into a library. It occurs when materials are acquired through purchase or donation. It also covers the spending of money (or encumbering of funds) and the actual receipt of physical material. Every library is going to have a slightly different process for purchasing books.

Monitoring the acquisition process is important because this is where a relatively large portion of a library's operating budget is spent. In other words, well-structured acquisition is a key component to demonstrating responsibility with public funds.

Library material can be acquired from many sources. Quite often a library has established vendors or distributors with whom they choose to work. There may also be limitations or restrictions on adding new vendors. Seldom do any changes to vendors or workflow need to be made to accommodate graphic novels. Many popular library suppliers are beginning to include graphic novel titles in their catalogs.

When choosing a vendor, remember to factor in cost, selection, and reliability. Other important things to consider are how returns and refunds are handled, whether previewing is permitted, and if any recommendations are available. These questions must be asked of each individual store or distributor you might work with because every company handles them differently.

Five Aspects to Consider with Graphic Novel Vendors
• Costs and Discounts • Selection • Returns and Refunds • Previews • Recommendations

2.2.2 Local Sources: Shops and Chains

Local comic book shops and bookstores are good sources for an initial foray into the world of graphic novels. In one stop, you can see what is new, inquire about what is popular, and get an idea of prices and selection.

When possible, there are benefits to working with local shops, although it may be financially or logistically prohibitive to use them as a major source of materials. In that case, include graphic novels in the regular orders through standard suppliers, but make a point of including your local stores in your purchases whenever possible. Purchasing locally shows the library's support of the community and balances this support with financial responsibility. In addition, local shops may appreciate extra promotion if they are offered an opportunity to present an informational program at the library. Work together to find an interesting topic, invite the teens, and make an evening of it.

Local comic book shops and bookstores are very good acquisitions options for libraries in mid-sized to large cities. Some tips to find local comic book stores include:

- Look in your local phone book's yellow pages under "books" or "comics."
- Check out malls and plazas in your area.
- Diamond Comic Distributors maintains a Comic Shop Locator Service on their Web site (csls.diamondcomics.com) and through the toll-free number 1-888-COMIC BOOK (1-888-266-4226).

One of the most recommended methods used to locate reliable stores is to ask the teens at your library where they buy their comics!

Working with Local Stores: PLUSES

- The staff of comic stores are likely to be experienced with the format.
- Books can sometimes be browsed prior to purchase.
- Purchases are instantaneous—no shipping delays.
- Retailers are likely to be very current with new releases.
- Local business owners have both the latitude and incentive to support their library with donations, discounts, or other contributions.

Working with Local Stores: MINUSES

- Discounts, when available, may be less than the going library rate among the more competitive distributors.
- The quality of advice varies from employee to employee, store to store.
- The selection may be limited.

Questions to Ask When Choosing a Local Vendor

1. Is our library's preferred method of spending money acceptable? Do we have to use checks, credit accounts, credit cards, or purchase orders?
2. Will our library allow direct purchases of material with later reimbursment?
3. Does our library have written policies or procedures for working with local vendors or for making outside purchases from nonlibrary suppliers?
4. Can the shop special order? Are there extra fees?
5. How are returns and refunds handled?
6. Are we able to preview material?
7. Is the sales staff available to assist a library representative in selecting appropriate material?

How to Tell If You're in a Good Bookstore or Comic Shop

1. Is the staff knowledgeable? Do they make suggestions to the shopper by, for example, showing them where a particular series is displayed?
2. Is the material displayed attractively? Are the books undamaged and clean? Is browsing permitted, or are all materials hermetically sealed?
3. Are prices clearly marked?
4. Is comparative space given to graphic novels in relation to comic books or other types of merchandise?
5. After you introduce yourself, does the idea of your library being a regular customer inspire interest in the staff or manager?

6. Is the store willing to give the library a discount?
7. Does the store have a wide range of titles available? Is the staff willing to special order? Are there any extra fees for special orders reasonable?

If the answers are *yes,* then you have made a good choice! Foster this relationship!

2.2.3 Shipping Sources: Distributors and Jobbers

Distributors, or "jobbers," offer an important service to busy libraries. They provide one-stop shopping for a library's collection because they work closely with many different publishers to promote and distribute materials.

With the many businesses operating on the Internet, traditional library distributors like Ingram and Baker & Taylor are now competing with online retailers like Amazon.com. While having a long-distance relationship with a vendor is often required for smaller libraries, any organization can benefit from the wealth of promotions and discounts offered by these large resellers and distributors. There are many options for finding vendors that ship graphic novels. Some recommended vendors are:

- Baker & Taylor (www.btol.com)
- Ingram Library Services. (www.ingramlibrary.com)
- Diamond Comics Distributors (bookshelf.diamondcomics.com; aggressively targets libraries with a special section on their Web site).
- BWI (www.bwibooks.com).
- Third Planet Comics & Games (www.graphicnovels.com).
- Amazon.com (www.amazon.com). Many GNs have "graphic novel" as a subject heading for easy searching.

WORKING WITH DISTRIBUTORS: PLUSES

- Many regular library vendors now offer selections of graphic novels. This minimizes changes to a library's existing workflow.
- Titles offered through library distributors are more likely to have existing cataloging records available for easy processing.
- Large vendors often offer appreciable discounts to libraries. For example, many offer a 20 percent discount and free shipping.
- Selections are usually more diverse than what is found in local shops.

WORKING WITH DISTRIBUTORS: MINUSES

- No hands-on browsing is available, so you must rely on reviews and recommendations for purchasing.
- Previewing is generally not available.

Questions to Ask When Choosing a Distributor
1. Is our library's preferred method of payment acceptable? Do we have to use checks, credit accounts, credit cards, or purchase orders?
2. Has our library worked with this distributor in the past?
3. Can the distributor special order? Are there extra fees?
4. How are returns and refunds handled?
5. Are we able to preview material?
6. Are catalogs available? How frequently are they released?

2.2.4 Summary

- Local stores and library distributors are two sources through which to acquire graphic novels.
- There are ways to recognize a good comic book shop or bookstore.
- There are ways to find vendors that are experienced with the needs of libraries.

2.3 CATALOGING

There has been much discussion over exactly *where* in a library collection to place graphic novels. Although the rationale behind item location is often an administrative decision, the day-to-day process of gathering the information necessary to add an item to the collection is the purview of catalogers. The decision of where to place graphic novels in your library's collection should be made *before* they arrive—and, certainly, before they show up in cataloging!

Comic art is a unique form of storytelling that can contain fiction and nonfiction topics. Libraries are accustomed to traditional books of text that are easily broken into categories of fiction, nonfiction, and paperback. Artwork in and of itself gets a nonfiction classification. Most GNs are released as paperbacks; do they belong in that section? Many of the stories are fictional; are all graphic novels fiction? These questions will be answered here.

One of the first rules of librarianship is to put the book in the reader's hands. Anything that comes between the reader and the book should be closely examined. Options abound, and libraries around the world are working to find what works best. Some important questions to consider before looking at the possibilities are:

- Which location in the library best advertises the new material?
- Which area puts the items in the hands of the most readers?
- Which section shows the most support of the cultural and artistic values in the collection?
- Which method of placement fits most easily into the library's existing workflow?
- Is there a willingness to try innovative ways of reaching the patrons?

We will now examine three approaches to cataloging and shelving graphic novels.

Three Things That Make Graphic Novels Accessible

- Include a subject heading of "graphic novels" in the catalog record.
- Provide patrons with a listing of graphic novels and their locations.
- Include graphic novels in thematic displays around your library.

2.3.1 Approaches to Cataloging

NONFICTION

Note: The Dewey Decimal System is used throughout this section because most school and small- to medium-sized public libraries utilize it as their system of classification.

A common way to catalog graphic novels is to place them in the nonfiction area. In the strictest sense, these books of comic art are indeed nonfiction. Placing them in the 741s is appropriate. It is convenient for the experienced cataloger and simple for the shelving staff. This approach views the comic art as the content of a book.

Considering graphic novels as artwork, however, is not without drawbacks. They are not collections of unrelated artistic images. Each panel in a graphic novel relates to the images around it and creates the illusion of an evolving scene. Will Eisner's definition of graphic novels uses the phrase *sequential art.* This is not the same as classic paintings by Picasso or Michelangelo. The images in comics are not entirely static, as in the case of most forms of visual art. A picture may be worth a thousand words, but a graphic novel can span even more. So, what does one do with a book of images that is not a photo collection, a book with words that is not a traditional novel? How would the patron perceive such a thing?

For the patron, the nonfiction area can be a maze of obscure numbers and apparently discontinuous topics. Remember the first time you encountered these walls of numbered books? Was the order immediately apparent, or did you wander around blindly until you found that one "secret code number" that meant your favorite subject? Until the method is understood, this maze can be confusing and a barrier to browsing by the not-so-avid reader.

When graphic novels are interfiled in the nonfiction area according to the topic of its subject matter rather than clustered in the 741s, the problem is compounded. Comic art is then sprinkled throughout the stacks, cataloged under the Dewey (or Library of Congress) number of its subject matter. Patrons and staff are forced to rely on the catalog to find graphic novels. In this case, opportunities for casual browsing are eliminated, except in the case of the most dedicated library users, or under the most fortuitous of circumstances.

Promoting graphic novels sequestered in the nonfiction area can be challenging. In the absence of visible signs of "something new," patrons (and staff) must rely on the library catalog to locate graphic novels among the stacks in the building. Under these circumstances, increasing awareness of a circulation goldmine like graphic novels involves bringing the collection out of the stacks and placing them on special display.

Shelving graphic novels in the nonfiction area will reach two types of users: patrons looking for a specific subject who may not want, or cannot use, a comic book version of their topic; and some teens who want graphic novels and nothing else—they will haunt the stacks until they find them.

In either case, be it by experience or technology, only dedicated library teens will check the catalog and venture into the nonfiction area. The novice library user who saw a friend reading a graphic novel is unlikely to visit this area spontaneously and may not request assistance from a staff member.

FICTION

Graphic novels placed in the fiction area have a better chance of circulation because this area is most often browsed for recreational purposes. Library users will scan the shelves looking for their favorite genre or a special author. This does not often occur in the nonfiction area. (Contiguous shelving of GNs is impossible in any area not exclusively dedicated to them.)

The benefit of fiction cataloging of graphic novels is that patrons will have an easier time of finding works by favorite authors. (This could also be a disadvantage for patrons who are unfamiliar with graphic novel authors.) For library staff, fiction cataloging is generally regarded as less complicated than nonfiction work, streamlining the cataloging process and perhaps getting the books on the shelves quicker.

Still, interfiling GNs in fiction, as with nonfiction interfiling, breaks one of the primary rules of marketing: If they cannot see it, they do not know it exists. Spreading comic art throughout a facility by mixing it with other non-GN collections does the reader a disservice.

SEPARATE COLLECTION

To be the most useable, a graphic novel collection should be just that—a dedicated space filled with unique material. Placing the material in a unified, distinct collection means that *some* comic art is shifted from the nonfiction and fiction areas and is placed in a visible, consistent location.

With this method, a library can catalog for call numbers and shelve by collection. Within a graphic novel collection, materials are organized according to call number. The fiction GNs will be organized by fiction rules, the nonfiction by its numbers; yet all graphic novels would be shelved in the same space.

Catalogers can process and label the items by their correct designations and can assign a collection designation of "graphic novel" or "comic novel" for the patron's convenience. They can label the spine with the proper call number and a sticker indicating the special nature of the content: Graphic Novel. The books can then be shelved properly *within* the graphic novel collection by their fiction and nonfiction labels. Many library supply catalogs sell labels for graphic novels on the same pages that offer other genre stickers. This indicates that many libraries are including GNs in their collections.

Staff and patrons can then look in a dedicated area for this collection, using familiar styles of call numbers to find the materials they need.

FINAL ANALYSIS

Busy, growing, changing—these words describe not only teenagers but most of our culture's adult population as well. A fundamental part of a librarian's job is to promote the enjoyment and education of reading. As many librarians have noticed, graphic novels support these purposes through their increasing popularity among children and teens.

There is only one place for a book to be—in someone's hands, being read and enjoyed. The best way for this to occur is for the patrons to *see* it. The recommended approach is to place all graphic novels in one collection. Some libraries consider them as young adult fiction, sequence them by author's last name, and shelve them together in a graphic (or Comic) novel section. Some facilities create a special place and collection for them and label the books as "Graphic Novels." This "separatist" philosophy allows the option of further division by shelving the fiction GNs alphabetically by author, and by shelving the nonfiction GNs by decimal number.

Dusting the graphic novel collection is not a phrase uttered by any library with a separate, fresh collection. GNs in a well-used collection are in more danger of disintegrating from use than they are from pages growing yellow with age. Some libraries, in fact, report that graphic novels circulate more than their young adult fiction—despite YA fiction outnumbering GNs by ten to one. Increased circulation can be a positive trade-off for creating a separate collection.

To be fair to the critics of this approach, graphic novels are not, from the traditional library perspective, a distinct format. When you "open the box" of a graphic novel, you see pages of paper. You do not see the magnetic tape of audio books or videos. You do not see the plastic circles of audio CDs or DVDs. You see paper and, upon those pages, artwork. Hence, by strictest definition, the material ends up in the nonfiction area cataloged as some form of art. Following this logic, graphic novels are not a unique format. At this fine level of distinction, credit must be given to library science majors. Yet the method of telling a story is only half the issue. Readers choose material for its content, and this is where graphic novels have something in common with other nontext formats, such as audios and videos. Unlike the standard definition of "art," graphic novels use their images to tell many, varied stories. Art books do not have a story to tell—they are not meant to be novels. Graphic novels, however, always have a tale to tell.

For nonfiction purists, there will come a day that brings a baffling cataloging conundrum. What happens when someone writes a "how to" book exclusively in comic art? Will it end up in the 600s, the 700s, the graphic novel collection, or the "to be returned" pile? A more practical example is Jay Hosler's *Clan Apis*. Written by a biologist, this book tells the story of a colony of bees, accurately describing their habits. Pure juvenile nonfiction, right? It is entirely done in comic art. Will it circulate more tucked away in the 500s or shelved in the 700s, or will it be more visible in a distinct graphic novel collection? The experience of many libraries is that the latter leads to the most use.

When discussing the merits of separate GN collections with librarians, one argument prompts filing graphic novels with the fiction or nonfiction areas. The notion of a separate collection for comic books was dismissed. The discussion posed the idea that if those books are segregated from the rest of the collection based on something other than format, then why not create a Stephen King collection or an organic gardening collection to accommodate the readers of other popular books? If almost all graphic novels are separated because they are popular, then librarians should follow suit and create special collections for all of their popular topics.

In this argument, the books under discussion are all *exclusively text-based*. Graphic novels do not rely entirely on words to convey a story. In some ways, though, this separation of popular materials has occurred. Readers often start out by reading a single book. They then discover an author and read as much of that person's work as they can find. This is followed by the realization that "their" author was not operating in a vacuum and the reader discovers genres.

When fiction is broken into genre, the loss to the patron of not finding the contiguous works of a diverse author is offset by any circulation increases obtained from offering genre readers one-stop shopping. This "separatist" approach places the burden on the library staff to organize material in a convenient, rather than completely logical, order. For the convenience of our patrons and supporters, this is what is being proposed by shelving graphic novels in a separate collection.

One of the first aims of a library is being able to get the book into the reader's hands. Placing material where "it ought to go" is shortsighted. Not every reader, particularly youths and teens, will use the catalog to locate items buried in the nonfiction section. Young readers and teens are becoming increasingly visual in their selection of material—if they do not see it, they do not know it exists. A dedicated and visible GN collection is likely to receive more use than would a few books of comic art filed in the depths of the nonfiction area. As such, it might be preferred to place the graphic novels where *your* patrons will find them! If that means calling them "fiction," "nonfiction," "paperbacks," or "comic novels," it makes no difference. If the teens can see them, they will circulate.

If the library's target audience for a graphic novel collection is teens and there is a strong desire to catalog the collection properly, be aware that extra marketing may be needed to help it become popular. Here are some suggestions to consider:

- Pull titles out for display. This makes the items difficult to find after searching the catalog, but it increases browsing traffic.
- Maintain a listing. Compiling and updating such a roster can be tedious, but it allows the items to remain on the shelves in their proper positions, and it forces users to wander the stacks if they wish to browse. Make it obvious that you have graphic novels—that is the key.

2.3.2 Approaches to Age Levels

Some libraries order graphic novels selectively and classify them as juvenile material. This works well in many situations, but it is not without flaws. Depending on the layout of a facility, teens and adults who are interested in graphic novels will need to roam the children's section. Over and above asking a teenager to visit the "kiddie room," this reinforces the idea that graphic novels are only for children. In addition, many popular fantasy and Manga titles are definitely not for children. They are designed for teens and adults.

Libraries that shelve comic art material exclusively in the children's area are limiting the future growth of their collections.

When graphic novels are placed exclusively in a young adult area, most of the bases are covered. The collection is centrally located to the age group that is most likely to use it. Children and preteens may find it but if books with more mature themes are clearly labeled "YA," potential liability is minimized. The teen area is often available to adults who wish to browse, so accessibility issues have been minimized as well.

What about classifying all graphic novels as adult? That covers most of the liability issues, and it will still be accessible (and acceptable) to young adults. However, there are many fine graphic novel titles available for children. Placing the physical collection in an adult area limits access. There are ways to resolve this issue.

A few organizations actually have dedicated graphic novel areas in each age-appropriate section of their facilities. This means that some patrons will have to hunt through three collections, but for the most part, each type of book will be within arms reach of the readers who desire it.

The only question to ask is, Where will patrons look for them? Pick a location, market it in other areas of your facility, and enjoy your collection.

2.3.3 A Cataloger's Guide to Comic Art

Regardless of how your library chooses to handle comic art and graphic novels, the following guide will help you understand what you are looking at when confronted with comic art in its various forms. After leafing through a book, consider the following:

If it has no panels of comic art—
- It is a text-based book.
- This item is not in the comic art family.
- It is not a graphic novel.

If it contains panels of comic art, but it has text outside the panel border—
- It is an illustrated book; this item uses comic art to enhance its text.
- It is not a graphic novel.

If it has a set of four to six panels of comic art, and each set is not closely related to the previous/next set of panels—
- It is a comic strip compilation. This material contains comic strips, often compiled into paperback editions. Popular examples are *Dilbert* and *Garfield*.
- It is not a graphic novel.
- This should be available near the graphic novels.

If it is smaller than a magazine, is stapled, is usually a monthly serial, and is exclusively done in comic art—

- It is probably a comic book. Usually twenty-five to thirty-five pages, sometimes climactic episodes are released as a double issue, which may be thicker. Popular examples are *X-Men* and *Spider-Man.*
- It is not a graphic novel.
- This should be available near the graphic novels.
- Note: Some thin graphic novels may appear to be a comic book. The graphic novel, however, is usually a different size. Also, if the title is not part of a serial subscription, you can file it with graphic novels.

It is a paperback or hardcover, more than forty-plus pages in length, and has a continuous storyline that relies exclusively on comic art (and the text enclosed within it) to tell a story—

- It is a graphic novel.

2.3.4 Summary

- There are pros and cons to placing graphic novels in different areas of a library.
- There are several options for traditional, patron-centered, and age-appropriate cataloging and shelving.
- Use the cataloger's guide to identify the major forms of comic art.

2.4 COLLECTION MAINTENANCE AND DEFENSE

The popularity of many graphic novel collections can bring with it increased wear and tear, especially among paperback copies. Also, because of their very visual nature, these collections could be open to potential challenges. These are two of the several long-term factors to consider when starting or continuing a collection of graphic novels.

2.4.1 Maintenance

Graphic novels, like any library material, will require maintenance. Several areas of concern should be considered when arranging a graphic novel collection. Three areas concern risk to the collection: theft, wear, and challenges. Two other areas concern using statistics to determine the health of a graphic novel collection and options to consider for weeding a collection.

2.4.2 The Danger of Crime

Accessibility carries an inherent risk of crime. When the material is popular, the risk of theft increases. The danger of crime, in terms of a graphic novel collection, refers to outright malicious vandalism or theft. Not everything that turns up missing has been stolen. An item could be misshelved. It could have been left in the book bag of a student who was rushing to class and then mysteriously turns up in the book drop a few days later. To safeguard against vandalism or theft in high-traffic library collections, there are two simple and cost-effective solutions.

- **Close the stacks.** For high-theft graphic novel collections, moving the materials to a staff-only area is a very secure, albeit labor-intensive, option. To enable visibility, a photocopy could be made of the graphic novel's cover. Place the copies in sheet protectors and store them in a three-ring binder. The actual books are then kept in a staff-only area. The binder is placed on display, available to the patrons. Decorate it attractively to draw attention to your collection, or buy a poster to hang above it. Patrons can browse this catalog of titles, note their selections, and ask a staff member to retrieve the books. Combine this method with a check-out-only policy that requires items to be checked out even if just for in-library browsing—and the theft rate practically disappears. Many libraries use a similar method to safeguard their CD, DVD, or video collections. This method puts several barriers between the patron and the material and it protects a library's investment.
- **Keep the location visible.** Keeping a high-risk collection in a visible location is sometimes enough to deter casual theft. Keep the collection visible and monitor patron activity. If any suspicious activity is observed, take that opportunity to introduce yourself to the patron and offer to help him or her find what they need. This method is very inexpensive and can provide an opening for introductions and reading suggestions.

In actual practice, most libraries report only a slightly higher than average theft rate in their graphic novel collections. As with any area of the library's collection, a little vigilance can pay off.

2.4.3 The Danger of Wear

The goal of developing a graphic novel collection is to build a dynamic, well-used collection. For libraries, normal wear and tear can be seen as something wonderful. When a new book begins disintegrating after thirty circs during its first month, it has demonstrated its value! Replace it—buy two of them. If it falls apart, then it is getting used!

In the late 1990s, some publishers of graphic novels were using inferior binding glue on their paperback graphic novels. This may have worked fine for the collector or for the fan, who would carefully read the new treasure and then retire it to a safe shelf. In circulating library collections, however, it was a disaster. Very popular graphic novels literally fell apart after two or three loans. When librarians around the country petitioned representatives of these companies to improve their binding, the publishers modified their production process. Some publishers now offer reinforced bindings for graphic novels that can survive the rough-and-tumble world of YA circulation for a reasonable period. As the industry slowly adapts to the special needs of libraries, perhaps some day these same librarians will petition for graphic novels that have Tyvek pages and covers. (Tyvek is the smooth, unrippable, and virtually indestructible material used for heavy-duty envelopes and home residing projects.)

Extend Their Lives

To increase the lifespan of graphic novels, especially paperback copies, tape the spines with clear book tape and consider the benefits of cold-laminating the covers.

What is the average lifespan of a graphic novel? How long a GN will last before needing repair depends on several factors.

- **Size.** Unlike regular novels, the paper stock in graphic novels is generally thick and it is often gloss-coated. It does not bind to the glue backing as easily as the thin, uncoated paper used in most paperback novels. The result is paperback graphic novels that have a tendency to lose their pages.
- **Circulation.** After twenty circs, a novel will show signs of wear on its spine and corners of the covers, but it will still be in reasonable shape on the inside. Graphic novels, on the other hand, are less likely to show spine wear (the thicker novels being the exception). The key signs of wear will be by the corners of the cover and loose pages. It is extremely rare to find a paperback GN in excellent shape after twenty-five circulations.
- **Construction.** Paperbacks cost less, but they tend to lose pages faster than hardcover graphic novels. Most GNs are only available in paperback. Usually only the most venerable titles are released in hardcover. Some companies are now producing special versions of their graphic novels with a reinforced library binding. As more libraries acquire graphic novels, graphic novel publication will more closely align itself with the rest of the book publishing world.

Most of the repairs needed by graphic novels are classified as simple mending: replacing a loose page or reinforcing a spine. Mending can be reduced by cold-laminating transparent covers to the paperback GNs and placing the book jackets of the hardcover within a protective cover. While this does not strengthen the actual binding, it protects and reinforces the spine and cover of paperbacks, maintaining the new look to which many young adult patrons respond. Jacket covers protect the paper cover of the hardcovers, almost eliminating the need to ever patch a ripped jacket with tape, which is never a very attractive or durable mending practice.

A graphic novel collection may seem to need more maintenance than a collection of text novels. The trade-off to this is that the GN area is usually a higher traffic collection. A library will get more bang for its buck out of a two-shelf properly developed GN collection than from a ten-shelf YA fiction area.

Because of their potential for higher-than-normal use and their not-quite-made-for-libraries binding, mending of most graphic novel collections can be expected to occur more often than normal. Take this reasonable wear as a compliment—it means the collection is successful. When a book falls apart at the end of its young life, mend it or buy another, and let the circs keep rolling in.

2.4.4 The Danger of Challenges

When it comes to library materials being found inappropriate or unacceptable to members of a community, an ounce of prevention is worth a pound of cure. Because of the visual nature of graphic novels, care must be exercised not only for the appropriateness of the item's language, but also for its images. It is prudent to be prepared for possible challenges if your library has a sizable graphic novel collection. A few steps will help you prepare and, hopefully, forestall challenges to your graphic novel titles.

- In the proposal, include information about graphic novels to your materials selection or collection development policy.
- Post positive reviews for patrons to read.
- Support purchasing decisions with reviews and first-hand previews of titles that have the potential to be challenged.

Despite every reasonable precaution, it is possible for your community to express concerns about a graphic novel. Any item in the library can be open to challenge, but visual materials such as videos and graphic novels are often more susceptible.

When faced with a challenge, particularly from an emotional patron, it is important to remember some basic communication techniques.

- **Understand procedures.** Know ahead of time the initial steps needed to process a complaint. This may involve asking the patron to complete a form, or it could entail a referral to another person in the library. Be prepared to explain a basic outline of how your library handles challenges to its holdings.
- **Remain calm.** Patrons initiating a challenge have a concern. Sometimes they feel that they, or their family, are being threatened by "improper" material. Another common concern is for the community at large. Allow the patron an opportunity to express him or herself in a reasonable manner.
- **Actively listen.** Focus on the patron. Consider his or her perspective. Do not offer opinions or counter an emotional argument with an objective discussion of library policy. Demonstrate comprehension by nodding and ask open-ended questions to clarify key points.
- **Offer assurances.** Let the patron know that something can be done. When appropriate, instruct the patron about the library's method of responding to the community's concerns.

Most challenges to graphic novels occur when stories containing images for more mature audiences are available to young adult or juvenile patrons. Many of these can be remedied with careful selections and cataloging. This is where a strong collection development policy comes into play. Graphic novels can enhance a library's collections, meet recreational needs of young adults, and offer many other benefits to a public or school library collection. A graphic novel can be more easily defended if it has positive reviews, if it is labeled for the appropriate age level, and if it is shelved in the appropriate collection.

2.4.5 Determine the Value of a Collection: Statistics

Circulating materials to its patrons is the lifeblood of any library. This is where hard numbers are generated that demonstrate how the community is being served. Statistics are also used to determine borrowing trends; the library can use this data to meet the needs of its patrons. In terms of funding, the collections that get used the most often receive the most new material.

In some ways, circulation statistics can be misleading when it comes to determining the actual value of the library's collections. Monthly or annual numbers of a collection's use give a clear picture about which areas of the library are generating the most check-outs, but they do not indicate which collections are working overtime to bring in the business. Most library statistics reports are aggregates. They do not factor in collection size. It is not unheard of for small collections that take up only a few shelves to generate circulation equivalent to stacks of other material. These small over achievers need to be identified, supported, and exploited.

These special statistical reports track the growth and health of any library collection, but they are particularly useful when examining smaller collections. When these techniques are used in relation to a pilot collection, they can help justify expanding to a full graphic novel collection.

There are two ways of looking at the same question: Which collection is working the hardest to bring in the business? Both reports allow you to optimize the layout of rooms and to identify which areas require increased marketing.

- **Circs-Per-Shelf.** This report will show you which collections are generating the most circulation relative to the physical space of each area. Circs-per-shelf is a quick way to estimate the over-achievers in a facility. It can be done quickly and informally.
- **Collection Turnover.** This report compares the number of items in a collection with its number of loans. Collection turnover requires an accurate accounting of a collection's holdings, something best obtained from your automation system. It may require involving other people or departments to gather some of these numbers.

No advanced knowledge is needed for these simple reports. All that is needed for the calculations are paper, pencil, calculator, and a copy of recent circulation reports that list the activity of each collection. For the circs-per-shelf report, the actual field work of surveying and counting the shelves is a great task for teen volunteers. The collection turnover requires basic math skills, something a teen library assistant might enjoy. Get your future librarians involved in more than just shelf reading—show them not only *how* the library operates, but *why* it does what it does!

CALCULATING CIRCS-PER-SHELF (CPS)

1. Count how many shelves are assigned to each collection.
2. Divide the amount of circulation for the collection by the number of shelves to determine the circulation-per-shelf.
3. Sort the list by circs-per-shelf, with the highest values at the top.

The CPS of your collections indicates which spaces are being used the most. This is a more accurate reflection of the traffic in an area than the straight statistics. For example, consider the information gathered in the following table.

Circs-Per-Shelf Example			
Collection	Shelves	Period Circ	Circs-Per-Shelf
Graphic Novels	3	200	67
YA Fiction	20	500	25
Juvenile Nonfiction	40	900	22.5

When you sit down to look at the statistics for this department, a cursory glance at the "Period Circ" column indicates that Juvenile Nonfiction and Young Adult Fiction are the big "money makers," right? Almost.

It should not be surprising that the nonfiction area has the most activity—it takes up forty shelves. If this area holds about thirty-five books on each shelf, then it has an estimated 1,400 items available for loan. Of course, a collection that size will bring in business. This collection, however, only generates 22.5 circs-per-shelf—the lowest value in the table.

That lowly bunch of comic books shoved over on the corner spinner rack, however, does not seem to be doing that great. Two hundred circs, versus nine hundred for juvenile nonfiction? An initial reaction might be to just get rid of them and to use that space as overflow for the burgeoning nonfiction area. But look at the numbers again. The CPS for Graphic Novels is 67 while the Juvenile Nonfiction's CPS is only 22.5. Each shelf of graphic novels is circulating almost three times as much as a shelf of nonfiction. If a library is looking for a place to invest when trying to build circulation, consider what six shelves of graphic novels would do.

CALCULATING COLLECTION TURNOVER (CT)

1. Determine the actual number of items in a collection.
2. Divide the amount of circulation for the collection by the number of items to determine the percentage of collection turnover.
3. Sort the list by collection turnover, with the highest values at the top.

The turnover of a library's holdings indicates which collections are being used the most. Consider the information gathered in this next table.

Again, observe that "Period Circ" does not tell the whole story. Juvenile Nonfiction is still in the lead while the Graphic Novels are trailing far behind. Yet when the statistics are examined from the perspective of how much of each collection has circulated (collection turnover), the situation becomes inverted.

Collection Turnover Example			
Collection	Number of Items	Period Circ	Collection Turnover
Graphic Novels	105	200	190%
YA Fiction	600	500	83%
Juvenile Nonfiction	1,400	900	56%

Consider that these circulation figures were based on one month's statistics report. In that single month, Graphic Novels experienced an almost 200 percent turnover. This means that each item in the collection checked out *twice*. Compare this to the nonfiction collection, which would need *four times* that amount of time to achieve the same degree of turnover.

FINAL THOUGHTS ON STATISTICS

When you review your own results using these methods, there are no strictly good or bad numbers. This method will show your collections in a new light, each area reflecting its own merit. You may find that a ten CPS is acceptable, or it could be that your goal is to have key areas developed until they exceed a 75 percent turnover each quarter. These valuations are relative to the activity of your own collections.

Here are three suggestions to improve the collections that score low on these special reports. Try freshening the appearance of the shelves by weeding out frayed (or just plain ugly) items and replacing them with newer materials. Consider relocating the collection to a more visible position. Use target-marketing tools, such as flyers or advertising, to inform segments of your community about your collections. More information about promoting your graphic novel collection can be found in **3.1: Marketing**.

Improving Graphic Novel Circulation
• Freshen appearance through selective purchasing, weeding, and replacements.
• Change physical location of collection to improve visibility.
• Target-market the collection to segments of your community.

To use these valuation methods most easily, the graphic novel collection must have its own collection designation. Circulation statistics must be obtainable for this area. If collection-specific statistics are unavailable, the only way to generate these reports is to sample the use counts manually for each item in the collection. For example, if use counts were read at the beginning of the month, the old count can be subtracted from the new use count. This would supply you with the circulation of that particular graphic novel. Add them all up and the result is circ for the collection. This process is useful for periodically surveying the circulation of a collection that has no separate statistical designation.

Do not use these statistical methods haphazardly. Numbers floating in a vacuum are useless. Spot check the value of a collection throughout the year, every quarter, or annually. This will develop a sequence of numbers that provides comparisons to accurately track growth and value. These techniques can also help put both budgeting and marketing in perspective.

2.4.6 Growing Pains: Weeding and Relocation

Eventually every collection needs to be updated. Books wear out, and older, less popular material must make way for new additions. Weeding a graphic novel collection is necessary for several reasons.

First, removing worn items improves the appearance of the shelves. (This is a huge marketing plus!) Second, space is finite. Weeding allows the library to present the best collection possible with the most efficient use of space. Third, some materials become dated or unpopular. When they reach their end of life, they become dust collectors and sit on the shelves, circulating no more.

Removing items from a collection can be difficult. The best way to weed is to have firm guidelines in place and to be frugal, yet ruthless. Common guidelines used for weeding collections are:

- **Worn.** Cracked and taped spines render a collection colossally unattractive, particularly to younger patrons. Even if the book covers and pages are pristine, spine-out shelving presents the worst area of the book to scrutiny. Weigh carefully the book's recent use against its detracting appearance on the shelves.
- **Space.** Sometimes there is simply no more room to squeeze one more item on the shelves. There may be no place left to shift the shelves, and every extra nook is filled to capacity. The first things to go in this situation are multiple copies. If space is truly at a premium, consider discarding any duplicate copies, regardless of how well they circulate.
- **No-Use/Low-Use.** The great weeding dilemma is what to do with older titles that are no longer being used yet should be kept. Its time to promote

them for one last gasp at circulation. Find a gimmick or theme to promote these titles, such as "Books from the Bottom Shelf" (see **3.1: Marketing**). Admit to the teens that the items are on the way out. Create a "Last Chance to Read" display, filled with no-circ/low-circ items that are candidates for discarding. If an item is checked out, shelve it normally when it returns and consider it reprieved. Any books still in the display at the end of the month can be discarded with impunity. Another idea is to place a piece of paper in the book and ask students to read the book and take notes. Ask the reader to explain why the book should be kept or pitched. Perhaps a reading teacher could give bonus points for this "civic duty" reading. See **3.1: Marketing** for more promotion and display ideas.

When every effort to give the books one last chance has been exhausted, change the audience. Remember the adage, "What works over there, may not work here." Exchange them for an equal number of little-used titles from another branch or organization. As long as the books are in fair condition, and processing labels are similar, this can freshen the collections of both libraries with different titles. Low-use graphic novels could be traded with local comic shops that offer used books.

When the weeding is over and relocation has been given a try, its time to get rid of the dead wood. Simply follow the library's procedures for disposing of weeded material. Perhaps they could be given to the teen advisory group to hold a graphic novel book sale. (Be sure to request a donation to purchase more graphic novels for the collection!)

As with any library collection, maintaining a set of graphic novels does not end when the book checks out—it only begins. Theft, mending, weeding, and challenges can occur.

2.4.7 Summary

- Theft is a consequence of popularity. Loss can be managed.
- Wear is a consequence of use. Budget for replacements.
- Challenges can be managed.
- Statistics can indicate a collection's value.
- Growing collections require maintenance.

3

Promoting Graphic Novels

3.1 MARKETING

Marketing and promotion are a requirement for most modern libraries. They draw new visitors and help patrons become informed about its services and materials.

3.1.1 Why Libraries Should Promote

Promotion brings library material and services to people's attention. It lets them know what is available, be it new or old. For example, some consumers are visual and if they're inexperienced patrons, they may assume that if they do not see something, then the library must not have it. If they hit upon the sports section and do not find a title that specifically says "history of baseball," they may simply walk on. What if, however, they noticed a sign saying, "Don't see what you need? Ask at the desk!" The patron would then be informed about, and directed to, where to proceed for help. This simple sign is a marketing tool—it speaks to patrons who are having difficulty locating material, and it promotes the staff as a solution.

Some regular library patrons, particularly teens and children, may not be aware that material can be held for them. The simple act of mentioning "Would you like me to set this title aside for you when it comes back?" is a powerful promotional tool that educates your visitor about a basic service. This is definitely a case of building circulation with the basics.

These examples presuppose that a patron is actually *inside* the facility. How can libraries bring in new business? This is the realm of marketing. Marketing involves identifying how the library can meet specific needs and interests of specific segments of the population. In a public library, these populations could be high-school teenagers, parents, teachers, business people, or gardeners—*any* section of the community. Similar segments of a community also exist in a school library. Are the materials for ninth-grade students different from those needed by twelfth-graders? Do teachers need a collection of professional resources and journals? These are but a few members of the population who can benefit from marketing efforts by a school library.

This chapter will focus on techniques to promote and market graphic novels to teens. Many of these same techniques can be used to promote other library materials and services to other communities as well.

Three Parts of Good Marketing
• Physical Location.   • Informational Documents.   • Verbal Communication.

3.1.2 Inside Promotions

Marketing has three components: merchandising (physical location or placement), documents (information), and communication.

MERCHANDISING

One part of marketing is called *merchandising*. Merchandising is the appropriate placement of materials to maximize their use. Used in retail stores for decades, it involves understanding how people use a facility, where they travel, and what they see. Book displays are a common merchandising technique. *Inside merchandising* focuses on the actual arrangement of departments (or collections) to maximize their use.

Consider a grocery store. A customer may just run in for a second to get a gallon of milk. Milk and other staples are often located around the perimeter or in the middle of the store. This location forces the customer to travel past in-aisle displays, end-rack displays, and dozens of sale stickers just to get to the milk section. When the customer gets the milk, he or she has to navigate the store again to check out. The cash-register aisles are quite often masterpieces of merchandising. Displays, eye-catching signs, myriad impulse items are all crammed into these areas in a last-ditch effort to get the customer to purchase one more quick thing. (Incidentally, these impulse items often have the highest profit margin of all items in a store.) In this grocery store, the owner is using several merchandising techniques to part the customer from his or her money. A few lessons can be learned from this aggressive inside marketing style:

- Necessary items are in the rear.
- Sales and special offers are in between.
- Standing in line is a chance to buy.

How can this be adapted to a graphic novel collection in the library? Consider these ideas for displaying and promoting your new collection.

- Locate the graphic novel collection in a high-traffic, high-visibility area.
- Cross-promote the collection—display graphic novels in several locations around the facility.
- Display graphic novels face-out. Let the colorful cover art attract readers.
- Display graphic novels where the teens are. Place them near music CDs, magazines, or computer workstations.
- Promote graphic novels in your library newsletter or in the school magazine. Explain what graphic novels are, and list some new titles.
- Create book talks or activities centered around graphic novels. For more ideas, see **3.2: Programming**.

Draw Attention to Displays with Realia
• Drape attractive fabric behind or beneath the books. • Accent a display of nature or gardening books with a vase of silk flowers. • Hang a baseball hat next to a set of sports books. • Purchase a few popular comic books and arrange the covers into an eye-catching background for a graphic novel display. • Do not forget to include books, audios, videos, and graphic novels in the displays!

- Involve the teachers. Explain what graphic novels are and how they can be used in the classroom. See **3.3: Education** for more details.

Promoting graphic novels that are sitting on the shelf is not difficult either. Publishers often pay a great deal of attention to the attractiveness their book covers. Use them. Turn a few graphic novels on each shelf to face out. Let the book sell itself. Other ideas for displaying books and graphic novels are:

- **Not Just Superheroes.** Pull any non-hero graphic novel to show that heroes in comic art do not have to have super powers. Choose a mix of genres to show how well rounded the collection is.
- **Get Graphic.** Place a display of comics and graphic novels outside the teen area to cross-market the collection to adults.
- **Read it! Hear it! Watch it!** Bundle classics together to encourage students to explore literature. Combine various adaptations of the classics— put the graphic novel, video, unabridged audio book, and the original book together.
- **Start a "100 Club."** Every graphic novel title that breaks 100 checkouts gets a special sticker to let patrons know how popular it has been.
- **"See Also."** Place a "See Also" note in graphic novel adaptations that refer the reader to the book or video of the same story. These promotional items can encourage patrons to read the full novel.
- **Display "Books from the Bottom Shelf."** Find items in your collection that have lower-than-average use or that are, literally, from the bottom shelf, back in that dusty corner, and give them some time to shine.
- **Show your Curiosity.** Drum up curiosity about the new collection by wearing badges with slogans like "Get Graphic," or "GNs WOW!" Another suggestion is to purchase plastic hats in bulk and put your slogan on a hatband.

Bringing books out of the stacks and into the light of day gives patrons a chance to see something different. Let every element of a display inform patrons about what the theme is and encourage them to take a book home.

DOCUMENTS

Collection location and displays do a very good job of demonstrating what a library has to offer. They allow visitors to actually see what is available. But how can small collections or special services be promoted? This is where information must be shared with the patron. This is the second component of marketing—*documents*. Documents allow the library to present information about a collection beyond its location. Flyers and bookmarks about graphic novels and lists of suggested titles can be placed throughout the facility (or given to patrons when they check out).

Throughout your facility, information promoting the library and its services can be presented to visitors on posters, on signs, on bookmarks, or in booklets. Presentation is vital when designing these documents. They must look professional. Fortunately, many word processing and desktop publishing programs allow computer users to produce attractive and inexpensive promotional documents. One piece of advice, however—with the plethora of clip art available, there is very little need to physically cut and paste. Adding graphics physically, rather than digitally, complicates the production process and takes away one of the greatest benefits of using a computer: There is no paper involved until the user hits "print."

What information should be put on every document? Always include the library's name, address, and contact information, such as phone numbers and e-mail addresses. If you have a logo, use it. If you have a Web site, promote popular and new titles on a special graphic novel Web page.

After patrons get their materials and visit a few displays, they arrive at the circulation desk. This area should be a wealth of information. Pamphlets and booklets promoting library services, hours, auxiliary groups (Friends, Teen Advisory Group, and so forth), and programs are often found here. Some libraries offer small gifts to patrons who borrow a certain number of items. Small key chains or trinkets can be obtained in bulk and given to visitors who borrow five graphic novels, or who borrow a graphic novel and its associated book or video. Do not always rely on patrons to take a flyer or pamphlet from the rack—have a stack handy to place in their bag to take home!

COMMUNICATION

Remember the third part of marketing: *communication*. The circulation desk is an ideal place for people to talk with people. Never *just* check out the material. Take a moment to see each patron as a guest in the library and remember some basic personal marketing techniques.

- Look your guest in the eyes and smile.
- Use the patron's name. If they are unfamiliar, cheat and look at their library card or on the computer screen. Be friendly, and address them by their first name. Let them feel welcome using the library.
- Notice what is being checked out. Can any complementary topics or titles be recommended?
- Mention a program appropriate for the patron's age or interest.
- "Up-sell" graphic novels. Place a popular title at the circulation desk, and ask each patron if they have seen your new collection.

There is one step beyond simple check-out communication: Become an advocate. Advocacy involves, quite simply, drumming up enthusiasm about a topic. Start the ball rolling today. Talk about graphic novels to everyone. Show them to children. Discuss them with teens. Explain them to parents. Share them with teachers. Use flowery language. Distribute statistics. Become a fanatic, or softly speak your feelings as a lone voice in the wilderness—use whichever method fits your style of promoting the collection, but promote, promote, promote.

Now, some may be saying, "But, I don't like comic books!" That is fair. Not everyone does. Here is the sticking point of advocacy, and the secret that no one ever told you: You do not have to like what you are selling. Be familiar with everything in your library's collections, and be prepared to promote any of it to everyone. A librarian's job is to "sell" books and information. Our jobs are no longer in the halcyon days when the doors of knowledge were flung wide open, and where one or two dedicated bookworms passed through. Today's libraries are expected to provide service in order to compete. We have to promote ourselves, because if we do not, who will?

You do not have to be the world's leading expert on literacy, art, or librarianship to be able to promote something. You only have to know your material. Arm yourself with a few basic statistics. Observe for yourself whether or not reading graphic novels is beneficial to students. Watch patrons wander quizzically through the stacks, looking for "something." Do they leave with a smile after a few moments of your time and advice about a good graphic novel to try?

This advice is not limited to graphic novels. Find any niche service in your library, be it a collection of teacher resources, the new bookshelf, or programs and events. Be the resident expert in *something* your library offers. Mention it to every patron. Even if that person may not need the information today, he or she may mention it to a friend who does need it tomorrow.

Be aware, however, of the limits of your knowledge. Do not over-promote something with which you are not familiar. When you have reached the limits of your knowledge, stop talking. There are often patrons who may be very familiar with a topic, particularly in the area of popular culture. Unless you have gone beyond advocacy into the realm of fan-dom, consider carefully the idea of discussing Manga with a teenager. If he or she is an avid fan, your ignorance could potentially embarrass you and may even damage your creditability. Instead, adjust your mind-set and use these patrons as sources of information. Take this opportunity to learn more about their subject of interest. Why is it fascinating? What is the best thing about? What is the worst? Taking a moment to relate to your patron, of any age, will foster more goodwill toward the library than any marketing scheme you can conceive. It will also arm you with an inside track on what to recommend in the future, and how to promote that subject. Ask these people what they are interested in, and adjust your recommendations accordingly.

By now, there are well-placed collections in the facility, attractive displays throughout, informative documents at the desk, and friendly, informed staff all around. These key elements create a platform to market items that are available and help match the book to its reader.

What about items that are out in circulation? Can they be promoted as well? Of course! The best collection in the library takes up zero space because it is out in circulation, being used. This is the ultimate test of marketing and advocacy—how to promote something that is not present. (Attention bookshelvers: Master the following techniques to keep your carts empty and save yourself work!)

PROMOTING UNAVAILABLE ITEMS

This special type of marketing is useful for items that are out in circulation, materials located at other branches/locations, and for items on order. How can you promote a book if you do not have the book available? Take requests! Never let the absence of a title stop you from promoting it. Here are some techniques to aggressively promote requests and holds for items that are unavailable.

- **Tell people.** There are members of the public that think, "If I don't see it, it does not exist." They do not know it is possible to place a hold on an item, or to have something saved for them. It is not unheard of for novice library users to be completely unfamiliar with the basic service. Inform them.
- **Teen reviews.** Ask teens to write reviews of graphic novels for your school or library newsletter or for a library-related article in your community newspaper.
- **Top-10 lists.** These work great on signs, bookmarks, and Web pages. They show what the community is reading and encourage the reader to

enjoy the fun. Lists also allow people to track their progress. (Some top-10 lists actually have boxes to check off when the patron has read the book.) *Do not forget to include the library's telephone number on the list, so patrons can call in their requests!*

- **New item lists.** Have a sign or flyer promoting holds on items that are "Coming Soon!"
- **Promote a Web site of the month.** Many graphic novels (and authors) have official Web sites that contain bibliographies, biographies, and title-specific activities. Search the Web for your favorite GN and its official site. Here are some examples to get you started.
  - Boneville (www.boneville.com), by Cartoon Books.
  - Official Bryan Talbot Fanpage (www.bryan-talbot.com).
  - DC Comics (www.dccomics.com).
  - Elfquest/Wolfriders Books (www.elfquest.com)
- **Master listings.** For smaller graphic novel collections, create a brochure that lists the titles in the collection, organized by genre. Include information on placing holds with your computer system, and do not forget the library's phone number for call-in holds. When a patron borrows a graphic novel, give him or her the listing of the complete collection.
- **Catalog it.** Create a catalog of new items in the graphic novel collection. Use photocopies of book covers to promote popular items. As new graphic novels are processed, make a photocopy of each cover. Place the copies in sheet protectors stored in a three-ring binder. Display the binder attractively, beneath a poster that promotes your graphic novel collection, for example. Patrons can browse this catalog of titles and learn of items that your library owns—even if some items are not currently available for browsing.

Whether making a top-10 bookmark or a sci-fi graphic novel brochure, always provide instructions for placing requests. "Don't See It? Ask a Librarian! If its out, we'll save it for you when it comes in!"

Be cautious when using library lingo, such as "holds" or "requests," particularly with teen patrons. Unless the patrons have been educated about library terminology, they may not understand what "placing a hold" means. The simple phrase "We'll call you when it comes in" is more likely to be understood.

The logical extension of over-promoting a collection is that nothing will be on the shelves, yet it will remain popular. The downside to this is additional wear to the items. In addition, items with longer holds lists can become undesirable if a few overdue patrons make everyone wait months to see the book. Have procedures in place to successfully manage request lists and to rapidly replace worn or damaged copies. Consider purchasing additional copies if patrons will have to wait longer than a month to get their requested book. The one-month wait time can be vital when dealing with younger patrons, who may be impatient waiting all summer for something they wanted to read when school let out.

No collection can meet the "empty-shelf" ideal, but these promotion techniques can help increase the use of the collection. This is where the library automation system can really help. Learn which tools are available to track items that have the longest holds list, which items have the highest use, and so forth. A fresh copy may be required, or maybe a quick mending session will give the book enough life to sail through the rest of the requests.

This "perma-circ" phenomenon is very idealistic. There will, however, be items that seem to sit in the graphic novel collection forever. What do you do with the books that are always on the shelf? Consider why they are in the collection—How old are they? How worn are they? How much use have they had? It may be time to weed the graphic novel collection. See **2.4.6: Growing Pains: Weeding and Relocation**.

3.1.3 Outside Promotions

Spreading awareness outside the library facility can be challenging, especially for smaller libraries that don't have a dedicated marketing staff.

Recruit advocates who will discuss graphic novels outside the library. Find teens interested in graphic novels and involve them in the process of acquiring and maintaining the collection. Youth empowerment is one way to encourage kids to tell their friends, "Guess what I get to do at the library!" Positive word of mouth is often one of the most successful methods of bringing new users into the library.

Leave the library. Offer to share book talks with classes in the school or with community groups. Incorporate graphic novels into the presentations to show the diversity of the library's collection and its services. Leave graphic novel bibliographies and promotional flyers with each class.

Use the media. Purchase ad space in local newspapers to promote new additions. Offer to write a weekly (or monthly) article about best-selling graphic novels. Do not forget to remind the community to telephone the library to request an item.

Contact Collectors clubs. Could the library host their meetings? Would their members be interested in recommending titles or in sponsoring programs?

And the best way to draw new people into the library? Offer a Program!

Start small with marketing. Practice a few techniques on small, specific areas of the collection, such as graphic novels or a particular teen genre. When you find which methods work best for your organization, apply them to any collection in the library.

3.1.4 Summary

- Marketing involves merchandising (physical location), visible documents and information, and verbal communication.
- Marketing and promotion take place both inside and outside of the library.
- It is possible to promote available items as well as "invisible" items such as on-order materials and items out in circulation.

3.2 PROGRAMMING

Producing programs and events that involve graphic novels provides a positive opportunity to appeal to teens with popular reading material. Contests, activities, and graphic novel programs can educate your patrons about how comic art is made and about the library's own collection. This type of material also allows public and school libraries to take advantage of mainstream media promotions by developing programs related to graphic novel characters seen on television and in movies.

3.2.1 Purposeful Programming

Offering a selection of reading material to our patrons is one part of library service. Another important aspect of youth and teen services includes programming. Programming can as simple as organizing a small event or activity, or as involved as orchestrating a season of thematic events with outside presenters. Contests, meetings, special events, storytimes, and reading clubs are common examples of library programming.

Why Offer Programs?
• Programs bring users into the library. • Programs increase awareness of library services. • Programs provide opportunity for education and recreation.

To fully justify a program, it should at some level relate to the purpose of the library. Does the event elaborate on elements of the mission statement? Does it meet departmental goals? How does it meet the needs of a community? Does it present the library to teens as a place of fun and friendship, as well as a space for learning? When teens gather in the library there is an opportunity for positive public relations. (Do not forget the most basic reason for programming—to show that the library can be fun!) Draw patrons into the building. The rest will follow naturally.

Should school libraries offer programs? The community and patrons of a school library are unique. The community, in this case, is the students and the faculty. One might say there is a captive audience! Look for opportunities to extend and supplement curricula with creative contests and activities. Offer an ongoing contest that students can enter independently, with a drawing for a small prize at the end of a semester. Host a display of student art. What about poetry reading during study halls? School libraries are often a step ahead of public libraries in one regard: It is difficult for a town to require its citizens to use the local library occasionally. With curriculum tie-ins and educational programming, a school library can be a required visit for most students. With a dedicated reason for service, school libraries can not only educate, but they can also help their students explore themselves, their school, and their larger community.

Programs bring people into the building. They entice casual users to linger in the library and give regular users a reason to come back. Events and activities show the community that the library is not just about books. They reinforce the image of the library as a community resource. Programs increase awareness of library services. If the program attendees are in the building, they are learning about the library. Consider things that are observed as patrons walk through the facility.

- Did they pass by that display of new paperbacks?
- Did anyone stop to read the sign about blood-pressure screenings being offered by a local hospital?
- Did the visitors see library staff assisting other patrons?
- In passing, did anyone glance at the shelves of videos and murmur, "I didn't know the library had those!"
- Last, but not least: Did they see the graphic novel display?

These are examples of passive promotion—objects like displays and signs that offer service and materials without direct staff involvement. Extend promotion through programming with these suggestions:

- At the end of every program, offer to give a brief tour of your facility.
- Distribute bookmarks or flyers listing "further reading" related to the theme of the event.

- Have a small display of program-related items available for immediate borrowing. Solicit holds on the material by explaining to attendees that they do not have to read only what is on the shelves. You might be surprised at how many members of the public are not aware that material can be requested over the phone, or that if an item is out, it could be set aside for them when it returns.
- Some members of the public may be unfamiliar with the basic services offered by a library facility, such as the ability to request items via the telephone, or having an item held until they can pick it up.

Any time the community is drawn into a library, there is a chance to show what is available at the library.

Programs provide opportunity for education and recreation. Library patrons can be generalized into three categories: Those who visit because they need to, those who visit because they want to, and those who keep coming back because they love to. Programs entertain avid readers, encouraging them to revisit the old and explore the new. "Book Buddy" programs encourage older students to help children practice their reading. Computer classes give teens a chance to learn and teach new skills about technology. Programs help share materials, services, and ideas in the process of meeting patrons' needs.

WHAT KINDS OF PROGRAMS CAN BE OFFERED?

One popular catchphrase in business is "location, location, location!" For library service, the phrase should be "audience, audience, audience!" Library programming means going where the audience is and offering a mix of what patrons want blended with what is needed. Observe the ages and interests of patrons in your facility. Ask what they would like the library to offer. If students are not visiting the public library, then the public library could go to them with in-class book talks, career day speakers, or in-class storytimes. Take these opportunities to find out why students are not using the library. Are they meeting their information needs elsewhere? Are they familiar with how the library can help them?

Another thing to consider when programming is the level of audience interaction. This can be broken into three areas: active, passive, and independent.

- **Active participation.** These are often structured programs in which the audience must be physically or verbally involved in the activity. Some examples would be craft programs, book discussions, or an evening of tabletop miniature golf.
- **Passive participation.** These structured programs generally involve less action on the part of the audience. They focus more on listening. Storytimes or book talks could be considered passive programs.

- **Independent participation.** These programs allow patrons to participate at their own pace and do not often require active participation of library staff beyond the planning stage. Independent programs generally
allow patrons a longer timeframe for participation. Contests, such as
"Guess how many jelly beans are in the jar" and interactive displays like
magnetic poetry are independent programs.

Some librarians refer to independent programs as "passive," because
there is little or no formal interaction, as there would be in a structured
event. Those who feel that independent participation can require just as
much thought and energy as attendance at a structured event have challenged this perspective. For the purpose of our discussion, "passive" is dif-
ferentiated from "independent" by the *type* of activity, rather than the *style*
of participation.

Graphic novels are used in programs and activities in much the same
way as with any book. Title-specific activities are downplayed for two reasons. First, if your library does not own that particular title, then describing
how to use it in a program is a waste of pages. Secondly, referencing specific
titles will immediately date this manual. When the title goes out of print,
as it invariably will, then that program outline becomes less valuable.
Rather than develop activities for specific titles, there will be outlines on
how to create programs based on your particular collection of graphic novels. Primarily, do what works for your facility. If you base the activities on
graphic novels that are popular at your library, then teens will be more
likely to participate.

3.2.2 Book Discussion Groups

Book discussion groups, or "DiGs," allow teens to get together to talk about
reading. A classic example of active programming, book discussion groups require the participation of both the facilitator and the teens. It is highly recommended that the facilitator of a discussion group has read the material
before the group meets.

When selecting a title for discussion, choose a graphic novel that contains
a complete story with rich character and scenes and that has a unique style of
art.

Most book discussion groups talk about the characters and scenes in a
story. The facilitator may ask open questions about the mood or imagery of
the book. The easiest way to start a conversation among the teens is to ask
them, "What did you think about . . ." To get started, use the questions below. For more ideas of conversation starters, see "Developing Critical Thinking" in **3.3: Education**.

TEN QUESTIONS TO ASK IN A GRAPHIC NOVEL DISCUSSION GROUP

- Who was the most important or interesting character? Why?
- Which is your favorite scene? Why?
- Was coloring or lettering used in the artwork to indicate special attributes of any of the characters?
- What questions would you ask your favorite character?
- What do you think happens after the last panel?
- What events led up to the beginning of the story?
- How would you describe the characters?
- Which pages best use the panel layout to help convey the mood or action of the scene?
- How would the story be if the main character looked or dressed differently?
- Did any part of the story remind you of another book you have read?

Discussing a graphic novel in a group setting allows for expansion beyond the traditional literary topics. Because graphic novels are a blend of text and artwork, the conversation can include art style, page layout, color, and shading. For some discussion points, see **3.3.4: Using the Language of Comics Literacy.**

3.2.3 Book Talks

Long a staple of library service, book talks use short summaries of a book's plot and characters to give a short "commercial" for interesting materials. Book talks are considered a passive program because the students often only listen to a presentation.

When including graphic novels in book talks, you not only let students see what the library has available to check out, you also inform the teacher and the teens that graphic novels are a legitimate and viable reading format.

Choose representative titles from at least two genres. This will demonstrate the diversity and range of your collection. During your presentation, show as much of the artwork as possible. Consider making a transparency copy of the cover for an overhead projector or creating a digital presentation to be projected. This will allow you to keep a group focused as you speak.

If you choose to pass copies of the graphic novels around the room for students to explore, consider including a sign-up sheet for students to reserve the title on the spot. This saves teens the extra steps of having to make a phone call or visit to the library.

3.2.4 Contests and Activities

Two more types of programs are contests and activities. There are many levels of complexity when designing these types of programs.

An activity teaches a skill. The reward for completion is usually the act of finishing itself. Craft activities fall into this category. The reason for completing the craft is to construct a tangible object. Activities are active participation programs, requiring the attention of the patron and librarian during the event.

Contests are the next level of activities. Usually independent programs, contests require a *challenge* and a *carrot*. The *challenge* can require skill or knowledge or be as simple as writing one's name on an entry ticket for a prize drawing. The *carrot* is the prize being offered. The reward for entering a contest is extended beyond the intrinsic act of creation. To determine winners, contest can have random drawings or have the entries judged. Another way to think of a contest is to consider it an activity with a prize.

Challenges should be age-appropriate, with levels that match the intended audience. Unless you are working with a specific audience, such as teens only or first-grade students, consider *inclusive programming*. An inclusive program does not prohibit any child from entering. It is broken into levels that allow students of any age or ability to participate on an equal basis. Inclusive contests and activities can involve skill levels ranging from easy—"Put your name on the ticket for the prize drawing"—to difficult—"Write a 500-word essay on 'Why I Want to Be a Super Hero.'"

The carrot should be not only desirable, but should also have worth commensurate with the skill level of the challenge. It is a waste of resources to offer a $100 prize in a random drawing. Rather, offer a challenge along with it. It might also be insulting to offer a fast-food coupon to the winner of a creative writing contest.

Any activity can become a contest. Provide clear, written instructions, a deadline, and a prize.

Playing games with any book requires a detailed knowledge of the story, character, and plot. Trivia-based activities are often popular and require some set up time. Before creating any programs, games, or contests, select a few popular titles (or even series) and look through them.

- Keep an eye out for proper names of characters and locations.
- Identify key events in the story and which characters are affected.
- Make a note of the title, author, and, if part of a series, the name of the series.

Gathering this information is a great project for a teen advisory group or for a few young adult volunteers. After the trivia is gathered, it can be presented in many different ways:

- Sprinkle trivia into book talks and discussion groups.
- Have a graphic novel trivia contest.
- Play graphic novel trivia games with the teen advisory group.
- Make graphic novel games available to the after-school crowd.

Creating contests for teens could be a book unto itself. A quick overview of the process can be summarized with the words *Design, Draft, Polish, Promote, Judge,* and *Award.*

1. **Design the contest.** Independent activities often work best with busy teens. Give them enough information to take home to work on the contest. How long should a contest run? Allow ample time for word to spread (thereby increasing the number of participants), and for teens to complete their entries. A few months is usually enough for small writing or drawing contests, while a couple of weeks is sufficient to reward regular patrons with an in-house activity. Have measurable criteria to choose winners. Will there be entry categories based on age or theme?

2. **Draft the materials.** Keep it simple. Do not have complicated rules—stick with easily completed forms and clear instructions. The activity must be fun. Be sure to include space for contact information—name, address, phone, school, grade, teacher, and so on. Not only will this make it easier to contact winners, it is also a great source of demographics and for marketing material or mailing lists.

3. **Polish the presentation.** Let the draft material sit for a few days. Return to it and consider how to improve it. Start with these questions.
   - Is there enough space provided for the project?
   - Are the rules clear?
   - Is there sufficient time allotted before the deadline?
   - Will there be enough time to evaluate the entries before the date the winners will be announced?
   - Does the contest material use as few pieces of paper as possible? Is the presentation of the documents neat and organized?

   Make any changes to the contest format, style, and documents. Once the contest starts, these papers will be representing the program and should provide all the information necessary for teens to successfully complete the project.

4. **Promote the contest.** As with any program, actively promoting an event is key to its success. Mention it to teens during your patron transactions.

Make flyers and signs to post around the library. Engage support from teachers and outside organizations that work with teens. Alert the press. Use every possible means to tell people about the program being offered.

5. **Judge the contest.** Judging should be done impartially when possible. Simple fill-in-the-blanks contests are the most easy to evaluate—the answers are either correct or incorrect. (These are generally then put into a random drawing of all correct entries.) Creativity contests, involving art or creative writing, can take longer to judge. These contest entries should not be graded. They are to be evaluated. One efficient method of judging entries is to use multiple passes through the material, progressively sorting more chaff from the wheat.

Tips for Judging Creativity

- Evaluate the material, not the person. Ignore (or remove) the person's name.
- Judge the responses on objective criteria when possible.
- When subjective evaluation is required, involve others.

---

6. **Announce and Award the winners.** Communicating the winners of a contest can take many forms. If the display of student's names is permitted in your area, post a sign listing who won in which categories. Extend the interest in the program and consider offering an awards ceremony for the students and their families, teachers, and principals. This brings different sections of the library's community together in a positive way.

There are many games and activities that can be adapted to graphic novels.

Contest Ideas with Graphic Novels
Make Your Own Comic
Create a Superhero
Finish the Comic
Guess the Graphic Novelist
Graphic Novel Trivia Contest

MAKE YOUR OWN COMIC

Provide students with a piece of paper on which four panels (rectangles) have been drawn. For an in-library art activity, leave these forms on a table with some pencils. Display the students' artwork around the library.

This can be built into a contest by creating an entry form with rules and photocopying it onto the back of the "panel" sheet. Give young artists some time (a few weeks to a month), and post the submissions around the library. Perhaps there could be two judging categories, an official "Librarian's Pick" and a "Patron's Choice." Give a gold star or small sticker to patrons who checks out a book and ask them to place it on the best comic. (This works best if the artist's name is not visible.)

CREATE A SUPERHERO

This great creativity theme can be extended to many disciplines. The major components of any great superhero are a special ability, a deadly vulnerability, a secret identity, a base of operations, and a villain. Provide ideas for possible super powers and let your teens express themselves. Some very good source material for creating superheroes can be found on the Web.

- Lee's (Useless) Super-Hero Generator at http://home.hiwaay.net/~lkseitz/ comics/herogen/.
- The Hero Machine Online Character Portrait Generator at www.hero-machine.com. (This one is worth checking out just to hit the "randomize" button a few times.)

After teens have decided on the specifics of the character, invite them to extend their creativity. For artistic teens, invite them to draw or sculpt their own superhero. Have a workshop to discuss superheroes, and provide material remnants to let teens create a superhero costume on card stock. For creative writing, ask students to create an original superhero and write a story about his or her origins or adventures.

The Fans Can't Have It

Fan fiction and fan art are popular topics with teens. Be aware that it is technically illegal to reproduce any artwork or stories that are copyrighted. So, be careful with any "Draw Your Favorite Character" contests!

FINISH THE COMIC

Give the first three panels of a comic and let the teens create an ending in the final panel. As part of a longer program, such as a graphic novel read-a-thon or a graphic novel game night, have the participants judge the funniest or most original ending.

GUESS THE GRAPHIC NOVELIST

Identify popular graphic novels in your collection and compile a listing of the titles and authors. Create an contest entry form that has the titles numbered in Column A and the graphic novelists lettered in Column B. Invite players to match the correct graphic novelist to his or her book.

GRAPHIC NOVEL TRIVIA CONTEST

This classic match-up game is perfect for an independent program. Make an entry form with two columns, the first column numbered, the second column lettered. Let the participants match characters to titles, heroes to villains, or locations to titles.

Activity and Game Ideas with Graphic Novels
Graphic Novel Read-a-thon
Graphic Novel Trivia Game
Graphic Novel Secret Phrase
Character Charades
Comic Categories

GRAPHIC NOVEL READ-A-THON

Bring out the chips, pull up a beanbag chair, and let the teens spend the day reading comics and graphic novels. Provide pizza and soda.

Some libraries require a parental permission slip for this all-day "lock-in" because the teens are expected to stay in a designated area of the library for the entire program. Provide rest breaks every hour, and give prizes to the teens who can read all day.

Have a Graphic Novel Game Night!

Choose several graphic novel games, and play all evening. Have small prizes for the winners of each game, with a larger prize for a random guest or for the player who scores the highest points. Have several graphic novels available for browsing!

GRAPHIC NOVEL TRIVIA GAME

This is an active participation activity in which players answer trivia questions and score points. In small groups, teens can play as individuals. With larger groups, divide into several teams. The game can be played as a traditional trivia contest with questions and answers or "reversed" and played like the popular television trivia game show *Jeopardy!,* with answers that must be in the form of a question. Correct answers score the number of points appropriate for the level of difficulty.

Number of Players: Three or more. In a large group, players can form teams, each team choosing a captain who will speak for the group. Each game requires a host. The host will read questions, keep score, and cross out squares on the game board as questions are answered.

Materials Needed: Game board laid out in a grid pattern: categories across the top, difficulty level down the left side.

Set up:

Suggested Categories: Authors, Titles, Locations, Characters, and Events. From the trivia information, determine ten to fifteen questions per category.

Suggested Levels: For each category, have five to seven questions ranked from the easiest to the hardest. The easiest question rewards one point, while the most difficult rewards the most points.

Sample Questions: Here are some suggestions for phrasing the questions in each category of trivia.

In the category of Authors, prompt for the correct author by naming popular titles he or she has written. Ask for an author's birthplace.

- The stories of *Dream, the Sandman* are told by this author. Answer: Neil Gaiman.

- Which Japanese author wrote *Maison Ikkoku* and *Ranma ½*? Answer: Rumiko Takahashi.

In the category of Titles, identify a book in a series by its number order in the series, or provide clues to a particular title by describing a key scene or character.

- Name the third book in the *Elfquest* series. Answer: *Fire & Flight.*

- Which story tells about an English teenager who runs away from home to get away from her abusive father? Answer: *The Tale of One Bad Rat.*

In the category of Locations, provide clues to settings of graphic novels by describing a memorable scene.

- In *Fire & Flight,* Cutter speaks to his tribe in this place. Answer: The Holt.
- In *Maus,* after hiding with other Jews, where did the Cats take Vladek? Answer: The concentration camp, Auschwitz.

In the category of Characters, identify characters through memorable events or by describing their special powers or tools.

- This person changes gender when wet. Answer: Ranma.
- Which superhero was resurrected after he died in a battle to save the planet Earth? Answer: Superman.

In the category of Events, provide clues to a scene by describing the characters and the title.

- In a novel by Joe Kubert, Ervin Rustemagic uses this device to send messages out of war-torn Bosnia. Answer: Fax machine.
- In this series by Jeff Smith, the Bone cousins get involved in a fraud to win what local event? Answer: The Great Cow Race.

Play

1. Draw lots to determine which player (or team) goes first.
2. In turn, each player (or team) chooses a category and a level of difficulty.
3. The host reads the appropriate question, and the player has ten seconds to reply. If the player answers correctly, he or she gets the appropriate number of points. If the player answers incorrectly, he or she loses the appropriate number of points. If the player does not answer, the next player in turn is allowed to give an answer.
4. The host places an "X" in the game board square for that category and level.
5. The player who answers correctly chooses the next category and level.
6. Play continues until all squares on the game board are crossed off. The player (or team) with the most points wins.

GRAPHIC NOVEL SECRET PHRASE

This activity is another example of active participation.

Number of Players: Three or more. One person must be the host. This person draws the game board, writes in the letters as they are revealed, and keeps score.

Materials Needed: List of authors, characters, titles, and locations; a writing surface, such as a chalkboard, a write-and-wipe board, or large sheets of paper taped to the wall; two dice.

Set up: From the collected trivia information, choose several proper names of authors, characters, titles, and locations. Provide a clue to the secret phrase by using the word *Author, Character, Title,* or *Location.*

Play:

1. The host selects a secret phrase and draws one blank line for each letter in the phrase. He or she also labels the phrase with the appropriate clue (Author, Title, Character, and so on).
2. In turn, each player can attempt to guess the secret phrase (if correct, player gets ten points) or roll the dice, total the result, and perform the action listed below:

Dice Total	Action
1	Guess a letter. One point for each letter revealed.
2	Guess a letter. Minus one point for each letter revealed.
3	Guess a letter. One point for each letter revealed.
4	Guess the phrase now. Twenty points if correct.
5	Lose a turn. Give dice to next player.
6	Guess a letter. One point for each letter revealed.
7	Give the dice to a random player.
8	Guess a letter. One point for each letter revealed.
9	Free Bonus! Pass the dice and get two points.
10	Guess a letter. Two points for each letter revealed.
11	Guess a letter. One point for each letter revealed.
12	Guess a letter. One point for each letter revealed.
Doubles	Perform the action, and roll again.

3. The game ends when a player correctly identifies the secret phrase. The player with the most points wins.

This activity can be adapted for an after-school independent program. With a minimal investment, the Secret Phrase game can be played by three or four teens around a table.

Set up:

- Make Secret Phrase cards. Divide a sheet of card stock into squares. In each square, write the secret phrase and the clue.
- Provide a writing surface. Stock the box with half sheets of paper and a pen, or purchase a stand-up sign holder with a plastic cover. This makes an excellent write-and-wipe board when used with an erasable marker.

- Provide the rules and a pair of dice.
- Place the game in a box, and make it available to the teens.

CHARACTER CHARADES

Graphic novels are often filled with exaggerated characters who lend themselves readily to a visual activity, such as charades. Allow teens free reign to choose their favorite character, or have a prepared list of memorable characters from a particular title or series. Each player, in turn, has one minute to use nonverbal clues that help the audience guess the identity of the character. The player who guesses correctly receives a point.

Just Throw Chocolate

For quick, impromptu games during TAG (teen advisory group) meetings or classroom visits, toss candy to the winning player rather than keeping score.

COMIC CATEGORIES

This old pencil-and-paper parlor game can easily be adapted for a contest, as well as be a good filler for a graphic novel game night. Create a form of seven columns and four rows. Label the columns with the letters G-R-A-P-H-I-C. Label the rows with categories like Titles, Author-Names, Characters, and Places. The object of the game is complete the grid with answers to each topic that begin with the letters in the word "graphic." For example, a character for the letter "I" could be Inu-Yasha. An Author for the letter "P" could be Pini, Wendy. Play as a group with the grid on a write-and-wipe board, or distribute playing grids to each team or player.

3.2.5 Speakers and Presenters

Outside presenters are, in some ways, very easy programs to sponsor. It can seem as simple as setting up a meeting place, introducing the speaker, and stepping aside. Much of the work, as always, goes on behind the scenes.

Finding a presenter is the first thing to be addressed. This can be accomplished in many ways, the first of which is to ask teen patrons what they would like to learn, or who they would like to see. Do they want an artists workshop? A chance to talk with an author? Incorporate their ideas into a file of possible presentation topics.

Check with comic shops to see if there are any local or regional artists who might be interested in speaking to teens at your library. Perhaps a university art department has a staff member who would like to share information on caricature or comic art.

Professional speakers or performers are usually very flexible and responsive to the needs of a facility. When a contract is returned, include a note describing the size of the presentation space, the positions of electrical outlets, and the names of staff members who will be hosting the event. Include specific travel directions to your facility. These courtesies will help make the guest's visit a positive one.

Sometimes, when the speaker is local and readily available, informal presentations are easy to arrange. Give a few weeks lead time to promote the event through your best marketing techniques.

A final suggestion for working with presenters is to include feedback from the patrons when writing the thank-you note. This helps them polish their approach. It is also nice to hear a few kind words, from time to time.

Before any library program, take a moment and prepare a handout to share with the program attendees. Provide information about the topic, and be sure to mention specific titles from the collection. Include the library's phone number so visitors can call back to learn more.

3.2.6 Summary

- There are many reasons why programs should be offered.
- There are three types of programs.
- Graphic novels offer ideas for book discussion groups and book talks.
- It is easy to create contests, games, and activities that are centered on graphic novels.

3.3 EDUCATION

One common adult reaction to children reading comic books is admonishments to "Read a real book!" While some graphic novels are bound editions of several comic book issues, true graphic novels are original stories told through comic art. These books are not exactly in the same category as monthly comics. The theme today, particularly in library circles, is to get the kids reading, get them reading anything. Along with the growing acceptance of graphic novels in library and educational settings, home-schooling families (and parents of reluctant readers) are discovering the inspirational value of graphic novels.

One challenge in any educational environment is how to stimulate students and inspire them to learn. Introducing graphic novels into the classroom is a unique way to meet this challenge. Educators can use graphic novels for both in-depth study and supplemental reading and to inspire reluctant readers.

- Graphic novels provide stepping stones to full-text classics that give challenged students a way to develop reading skills in a nonthreatening manner.
- Graphic novels give students a chance to explore visual literacy and to develop critical thinking skills.
- Graphic novels can present information about literature, history, and social issues in a unique way that catches the interest of reluctant learners.
- Graphic novels contain springboards to extra learning activities.
- Graphic novels can inspire challenged students who lack reading confidence, reading ability, or motivation for self-guided reading.

Graphic novel adaptations of classic literary works promote literacy by removing vocabulary and conceptual barriers inherent in the original texts, thereby providing access to higher concepts by younger readers. Granted, many high school students have been known to curl up with CliffsNotes and an illustrated classic during the hour before the big English test. While this is not an idea study method, these two resources can help students expand their understanding of a literary novel, and it can give challenged students basic comprehension.

Some students are visual-spatial learners, while others are visual-linguistic learners. Illustrated adaptations can fill in the blanks for key concepts that "picture" learners may not have gleaned from the actual text of the novel. All around, graphic novels provide access to a full range of literary and recreational genres in a format that young students and reluctant readers find appealing.

The study of a graphic novel uses many techniques familiar to English and language instructors. These disciplines, along with art instruction, are the logical first choices for incorporating graphic novels into a classroom environment.

At the most fundamental level of any story, examining the vocabulary, word usage, and text density of the graphic novel can develop textual literacy. Stories told through comic art have one additional area to consider. Text density, the amount of text in a panel or on a page, is unique in comic art.

After basic language usage has been explored, some examples will be provided to help assist students in developing critical thinking. Specific examples of how to analyze the story and the artwork of a graphic novel will be given. This chapter will close with various extension activities for group work in class.

Graphic novels can be used to support many areas of elementary and secondary curricula. Using comic art in the classroom is a nonthreatening and entertaining method of drawing students into the subject matter. When imagination is invoked, children have another way to connect with a lesson. This connection between student and knowledge is an important challenge to overcome in educational environments. Inspiring a desire to learn is one of the best lessons that can ever be taught.

READING FOR THE FUN OF IT

When students are asked to read a graphic novel or a comic book, many glance askance at their instructor. If a teen or child chose to read such a thing, it would be of their own accord, without pressure of being graded. "It's not to learn anything," one can hear them say. "It's just for the fun of it!" The use of material with such a reputation for enjoyment and for play value can be an extremely motivating factor when choosing graphic novels and comics for classroom use!

3.3.1 How Many Words?

Words are instrumental in comic art. While some panels display action or set the scene, most panels involve narration or character dialogue. What are teens reading when they sit down with a graphic novel?

There is a popular quote used to defend graphic novels as literacy tools that refers to kids reading 8,000 words with *realizing* they are reading 8,000 words. This anecdote refers to the *Tintin* stories, by Hergé. These stores are very text-dense for comics. One librarian, after scanning a *Tintin* book remarked, "Why didn't he [Hergé] just write a book!" His stories range between 8,000 to 10,000 words in each episode. In a three-episode anthology, there are more than 25,000 words. This is close to the number of words used in juvenile fiction novels, which run between 20,000 and 40,000 words.

Today's teens are not likely to immerse themselves in a story about the adventures of a 1950s boy-adventurer. In an effort to update this "graphic novels are good for literacy" belief, titles popular with today's youth were examined for their word counts. Please note that the counts in this study are estimates based on sampling many pages throughout each book.

- *Nausicaa of the Valley of Wind,* by Hayao Miyazaki. The volume studied had 271 pages and an estimated word count of more than 17,000.
- *Ranma ½,* by Rumiko Takahashi. At 203 pages, this volume contains about 6,000 words.
- *Elfquest #12: Ascent,* by Wendy and Richard Pini. The book is 192 pages long, with 16,000 words.
- *The Tale of One Bad Rat,* by Bryan Talbot. The book is 185 pages long and contains about 15,000 words.
- *Pedro and Me,* by Judd Winick. The book is 180 pages, with 11,000 words.
- *Bone: The Great Cow Race,* by Jeff Smith. At 140 pages, it contains about 13,000 words.

- *Pokemon Adventures #2: Wanted Pikachu,* by Kusaka. This book runs 44 pages long, with 1,000 words. Note that each issue of this series is little more than an oversized comic book. Popular with second- through fourth-grade students, the children would often borrow multiple issues at the same time. Four issues would roughly be 176 pages and 4,000 words.
- *JLA: New World Order,* by Grant Morrison. Its 108 pages contain more than 10,000 words.
- *Daredevil Visionaries: Frank Miller,* by Frank Miller. Its 192 pages have about 23,000 words.
- *Adventures of Tintin,* by Hergé. One story contained 62 pages and more than 9,500 words.

From this small survey, we can see that an average contemporary graphic novel is 168 pages long and contains about 12,400 words. The reference to *Tintin,* with its 8,000 words, while accurate, has been surpassed by several newer graphic novels. We can now safely state that teens who read a graphic novel can read more than 10,000 words without realizing it.

In addition to word count, another aspect to consider when evaluating graphic novels in an educational environment is the density of the text on a page. This can be calculated by estimating the number of words in a GN and then by dividing that number by the number of pages. Review the table "Words per Page Assessment" to see how the graphic novels surveyed ranked on this scale.

Words per Page Assessment	
Words/Page	Title
153	*Adventures of Tintin*
122	*Daredevil Visionaries*
97	*JLA: New World Order*
96	*Bone: The Great Cow Race*
85	*Elfquest #12: Ascent*
82	*The Tale of One Bad Rat*
64	*Nausicaa of the Valley of Wind*
62	*Pedro and Me*
29	*Ranma $\frac{1}{2}$*
25	*Pokemon Adventures*

Surprisingly, the superhero genre generally has a higher text density than other genres. Most panels display action, punctuated with onomatopoeia (the *zip!, grunt!,* and *oof!* that has become the trademark of comic art). Many would assume that this would mean a lower word count. Actually, a well-developed action story needs many pages and to be text-rich in order to explain the adventure through narration and dialogue. The result is a higher density of text than would be found in other comic novels that rely more on character development and less on action. It appears that reading stories about superheroes could be advantageous to literacy, after all.

Manga graphic novels are generally at the lower end of the text-density scale because the Japanese art style does not rely on narration in the same way American comics do. As a rule, Manga relies more heavily on visual cues to tell a story. Emotion and scene changes are conveyed through the stylized artwork and through emphatic text styles in the speech balloons. Therefore, the word count in Manga novels is lowered because the story relies almost exclusively on dialogue to motivate the character's actions. This is the opposite of American treatment of action-heavy stories. The Japanese perception seems to be that the reader is familiar with a character's history and personality, and that he or she understands why the character reacts in a particular fashion.

The words-per-page ratio falls dramatically when evaluating comic books. Most comics have 50 to 60 words on each of its twenty pages. The word count in comic books ranges between 1,200 and 2,000. Still, for students needing positive reading reinforcement, comic books are a good choice! To start with, they have a higher word count than, say, a newspaper article, and they are far more appealing to children and teens.

A useful tool for estimating word counts in graphic novels is to determine how much text is on each page and multiply that by a *density modifier*. To accomplish this, scan through the book. Consider how much of each page is composed of word balloons and narration boxes. Locate the appropriate density modifier in the table "Estimating Word Counts in Graphic Novels," and

Estimating Word Counts in Graphic Novels	
Apparent Text Density	Density Modifier
Very high	140 words per page
High	95 words per page
Moderate	65 words per page
Low	25 words per page

multiply that value by the number of pages in the book. This will give a fast, though approximate, estimate of the word count in a particular graphic novel.

Using this method, *Nausicaa of the Valley of Wind,* with a moderate text density and 271 pages, would have about 17,600 words. *Pokemon Adventures,* a low text-density book of 44 pages, contains about 1,200 words. A high-density story, such as *Daredevil Visionaries* at 192 pages, would have about 18,200 words. The classic *Tintin,* on the other hand, is a very high-density story of 62 pages. Its estimated count would be 9,300 words.

How do the number of words in graphic novels and comics compare to standard literary texts? Using the same method of averaging word counts, three juvenile fiction books were examined. Karen Hesse's *Out of the Dust,* with 227 pages, contained an estimated 27,000 words; Madeleine L'Engle's *A Wrinkle in Time* is about 42,000 words; and Karen Cushman's *The Midwife's Apprentice* has 23,000 words. Even the most ambitious graphic novels do not meet these word counts. While graphic novels may be text-poor in comparison to literary works, we must remember that they are using artwork to convey much of the mood and setting of the story. They are a unique blend of text and illustration. In addition, as one researcher of graphic novels put it, the students are reading thousands of words without *realizing* they are doing so.

The language in graphic novels can be studied the same as any literary work. In a classroom, consider the following exercises to build text literacy using graphic novels.

- Discuss parts of speech and language terms. Ask students to review the graphic novel and to list examples of onomatopoeia, metaphor, exaggeration, and descriptive adjectives.
- Invite students to construct vocabulary lists. Which words are unfamiliar? Which words contain the most syllables? What is the longest word in the story? Which words describe the action or situations that move the story forward?
- Compare a graphic novel adaptation to the original literary work. Did the artist faithfully represent the characters, mood, and action? Were any critical scenes removed or shortened? Did these changes alter your reaction to the story?

3.3.2 Developing Critical Thinking

As with text-based books, graphic novels and comic art are not passive entertainment. The reader must become consciously involved in the story. There is an expectation that he or she will assimilate the flow of images and words.

Interpreting this type of story involves the same skills needed to analyze any literary work. These essential concepts of critical thinking apply to any book being studied. Keep the following open questions in mind when exploring a graphic novel with students.

> **Awareness.** Recall facts, terms, and basic concepts from previously learned material.
> - When did . . . ? / Who was . . . ?
> - Who were the main . . . ?
> - When did _____ happen?
> - What colors were used to . . . ?
> - How would you explain . . . ?
> - Can you list three . . . ?
> - Who was . . . ?
>
> **Understanding.** Organize and interpret descriptions and main ideas.
> - What is the main idea of . . . ?
> - What scenes support . . . ?
> - How would you summarize . . . ?
> - How do you know . . . ?
>
> **Relevance.** Apply knowledge under different circumstances.
> - What examples can you find to . . . ?
> - What would result if . . . ?
> - What questions would you ask if you could talk to . . . ?
>
> **Investigation.** Refer and find evidence to establish motives and causes.
> - What motive is there . . . ?
> - How would you classify . . . ?
> - What is the relationship between . . . ?
>
> **Combination.** Mix existing elements to create a new pattern or solution.
> - What changes would you make to show . . . ?
> - How would you improve . . . ?
> - How could you change the plot to show . . . ?
> - Can you predict what happens after . . . ?
> - Can you think of another way . . . ?
>
> **Assessment.** Discern the validity of information based on a set of criteria.
> - Why did the character choose . . . ?
> - Would it be better if . . . ?
> - Could the character be drawn better if . . . ?
> - What choice would you have made . . . ?
> - Why was it better that . . . ?
> - How would you compare the characters . . . ?

Encouraging discussion is one important method of reinforcing comprehension among students.

3.3.3 Using the Language of Literature

Standard methods of studying literature can be used to analyze a graphic novel. The artwork enhances the experience by providing visual cues to the story. In addition to studying the mechanics of how the characters are drawn and the layout of panels on the page, students can interpret how the text and the images support each other.

One first step in examining any story is to explain the key elements of literature. Any story will often have the following attributes:

- **Characters.** The people and creatures in a story.
- **Setting.** The place and time a story happens.
- **Plot.** The sequence of events and scenes.
- **Movement through time.** The progression of characters.
- **Change,** or lack thereof.
- **Relevance.** Why are we reading it?
- **Theme.** What concept did the author intend to convey? Why did the author write it?

When discussing the elements of a graphic novel's story, other elements can be considered as well.

- **Character Interplay.** How do other characters relate to the main character? How would the story be affected if the main character looked or dressed differently?
- **Critical Choice.** At what point in the plot could the character have made a different decision that would have affected the outcome?
- **Who's Who?** Guide the students to identify gender and social roles through cues provided by a character's clothing and accessories.
- **Self-Analysis.** Encourage students to think about which characters they identify with, and why they feel that way.
- **Sequencing.** Ask the students to retell the story and to explain the sequence of events.
- **Theorizing.** Review the opening and ending scenes of the story. Ask students to consider the events that led up to the beginning. Ask them to extrapolate what happens after the last scenes.
- **Inspiration.** Encourage personal association by asking students if the story reminds them of any other story, or of another event. Use leading questions such as, "This reminds me of . . . ," "I noticed that . . . ," "I wonder why . . . ," "This surprises me because . . . ," or "This makes me think of another book because . . . ."

Of course, there is the perennial classic of literary interpretation: "What is the moral of the story?"

How to Eat a Comic

- Savor each page. Study the panel layout. Where does each sequence of panels begin? Does the layout provide direction on how to read the sequence?
- Nibble on each panel. Look at the image within. Identify speaker(s) and listener(s). Study the background. Look at how each object is drawn.
- Taste the words. Does the balloon and lettering provide a clue about the character's feelings? Does the text sound like what the character is expected to say?
- Chew thoroughly. Review the panels before and after, looking for similarities or differences in the artwork. How does each panel relate to the others?

3.3.4 Using the Language of Comics Literacy

Visual literacy refers to how people respond to information that is presented visually. This is an extension of "art appreciation." Knowing how to interpret images is important, but visual literacy is also concerned with how people comprehend information visually, such as the layout of text and images on television or computer screens, on pages of magazines, and even on boxes and bottles of household products like shampoo and breakfast cereal.

Visual literacy requires people to identify parts of an image, to comprehend how these pieces interrelate, and then to interpret the message presented. The image being studied could be a piece of artwork, a Web page, or, in this case, comic art.

Comics literacy is a form of visual literacy. In literary works, words are the only tool available to explain both the physical and intangible environments, such as location or emotions. Comics teach visual literacy by using artwork to expand on the text presented through dialogue and narration. Elements of visual literacy that can be explored through comic art are:

- **Identifying parts of an image.** What people, places, and objects are in the image? What is in the foreground or background.
- **Comprehending visual images.** How do the elements interrelate to create mood and implied movement and to focus the viewer on the center of attention.
- **Interpreting visual images.** What is the message? What information is conveyed? What style, or theme, was used? Is the message relevant to the viewer?

In comic art, visual interpretation skills are critical. The reader must understand how to decode the image in order to read the story. Another important skill is associating the text to the correct parts of an image, such as identifying narration and each speaker's dialogue. A reader's ability to interpret action and mood across discrete panels is also vital to understanding comic art. These skills help readers build visual literacy.

When studying graphic novels in the classroom, it is common to begin a discussion of comic art with an explanation of its basic components. Consider using, or adapting, the "Accidental Comic" in **1.1: Categories**. More elements can be added to the panel, the gutter, and the border to build a more complete understanding of comic art.

- **The page:** panel layout, gutters, and navigation devices.
- **The text:** balloons, typography, and color.
- **The image:** line, shading, perspective, color, and motion.

The page itself provides the first visual cues about the scene. Panels can be repeating squares, rectangles, or even abstract, angular shapes. Their layout on the page often gives the first clue about the sequence in which the panels are intended to be read. The gutters, or space between the panels, put visual distance between each piece of the story. They give the reader a small psychological break between each "frame" of the scene. If the layout of a page is complex, there will often be navigational devices provided—small arrows or lines to guide the reader from panel to panel. These devices are often used in more abstract layouts, especially those involving multiple character or places.

The text in comic art does more than tell the story. Comic art will often use different lettering styles to indicate how a character's voice sounds. The color of the speech balloons can indicate who is speaking. The shape of the balloons provides cues as to whether the text is being spoken or thought.

The images show the artist's style and how he or she felt the story should be illustrated. Lines can be thick, thin, or (in some styles) almost nonexistent. Shadows can be drawn in solid tones or with cross-hatching. Perspective places the characters closer to the reader or farther away in the panel's background. Color allows the reader to consistently identify characters and objects. Motion, usually shown through lines drawn in the foreground or background, allows the reader to follow characters through the artwork.

After explaining the basics of what to look for, discuss how the elements work together to strengthen the text of the story.

- How does the artwork help a reader identify each character?
- What elements of the artwork (color, line, shading) provide clues to the setting?

- How do the elements of comic art convey the action of the story?
- Are the events and scenes portrayed in a consistent artistic style?
- How does each element contribute to changes in mood or action?
- Do any characters have a unique way of speaking? Are their speech balloons shaped the same? Are they colored the same? Does the way the text is drawn provide clues to a character's attitude or emotional state?
- Are any panels unclear? Which panels contain the most vivid or descriptive images?
- How does the layout of panels on the page convey the mood of a scene?

After students examine a graphic novel for its literary value and study the artwork, then consider how the two interrelate to tell the story.

- How does the artist's use of color or shading contribute to (or hinder) the story?
- Examine how each element is conveyed through both the text and the comic art. For example, which clues exist in the text that describe a character's appearance or abilities? Does the page layout help to convey the mood or action of the scene?
- Discuss how each element is affected when the artwork is removed. Ask how specific elements rely most heavily on the dialogue or narrative of the story. For example, invite students to pretend they are reading the graphic novel "blindfolded" to the artwork. Using just the text, can they clearly "see" the elements of the story?
- How are the elements affected if the text is removed? Ask how specific elements rely on the visual images to convey the story.
- Invert the previous exercise and ask students to imagine the story without words. What do they imagine is happening? (Better yet, obtain a copy of a foreign-language graphic novel and invite the students to explain the images without the help of textual clues.)

3.3.5 Using Comics in the Classroom

Graphic novels and comic art are visual storytelling mediums. There are several ways to expand this with classroom exercises. These activities give students opportunities to explore how the words and the pictures work together.

The Picture Is Worth How Many Words? Select several panels of comic art that contain rich backgrounds. Discuss how the artwork plays a pivotal role in graphic novels. Ask students to write about the scene portrayed in a panel. Use descriptive adjectives to describe the environment. Use prepositions to describe relationships between the objects. Involve the senses with the smells, sounds, and sensations of that scene.

Describe the time of day, how the weather is. What is the character saying? What is he or she thinking? Feeling? Encourage students to write as much as they can to describe a single panel of artwork and the story it conveys.

Guess the Action. Give students a comic strip or series of panels from which the text has been removed. Describe verbally the scene contained in one panel and ask students to identify the corresponding panel of artwork.

Comic Tableaux. One reader tells the story from the book while classmates stand behind a rectangular frame that represents the panel. These students pose as they imagine how the characters would look in the artwork. These "living tableaux" give other students an opportunity to visualize the artwork, as well as to offer feedback on how the "actor" is performing. This exercise is great for group work when there are not enough copies of the graphic novel for individual reading.

"One-Eyed" Comics. Reproduce one or two panels from a comic book or graphic novel. Cut the text balloons out of the artwork. Place the text on one page, the artwork on another. Ask students to discuss their understanding of the story based on the entire panel, the text alone, and the artwork alone.

"One, Two, Three." Practice sequencing by providing students with a collection of unordered panels and asking them to place the story pictures in their correct sequence.

Group Work. When possible, provide multiple copies to groups of students. Encourage each learning cluster to examine and discuss the book, and to present their findings to the class.

Silent Comics. Develop visual literacy by relying exclusively on visual cues to interpret the story. Ask students to identify characters, action, emotion, and sequence of events. What makes the main character identifiable? Suggested titles for this activity are *Gon* and *Age of Reptiles*.

Design a Costume. Read and discuss graphic novels in the superhero genre. Discuss how the design of a hero's costume reflects his or her special abilities. What specific abilities would you expect the hero to have? Did the hero (or villain) exhibit any abilities or traits that your students found surprising? Extend the discussion into types of superpowers, and encourage students to design a unique costume. Involve multimedia by suggesting that the artwork does not have to remain confined to paper—fabrics, computer graphics, and natural materials could be used.

Trivia Wins. Test story comprehension by playing a game, such as Graphic Novel Trivia Game or Graphic Novel Secret Phrase (see **3.2: Programming**).

Comic art and graphic novels can also be used as a segue to language exploration. Consider using these activities to help students develop their language skills.

- Encourage them to describe characters using adjectives.
- Find synonyms and antonyms for terms within the text.
- Practice basic rules of pronunciation by asking students to take turns reading aloud.
- Exercise skills in direct speech writing by asking students to describe a series of panels using nothing but phrases such as "Hey, Mom!" and "Darn that cat!"
- Reinforce recognition of word reductions like "gonna" and "hafta" through oral recitation of the corresponding long forms.
- Explore time-sequence transition words to maintain story flow, such as "First, the girl woke up. Then, she . . ."
- Identify and explore paralanguage terms, such as "uh-oh" or "psst."
- Introduce onomatopoeia and identify examples throughout the graphic novel.
- Practice verb tenses by changing the language of a panel from present tense to past tense.

3.3.6 Recommended Graphic Novels for Classroom Use

Many titles on the market can be used successfully in middle and high school classrooms. Some suggestions are *Maximum Asterix, Maus: A Survivor's Tale, Fax from Sarajevo, Fallout, Clan Apis, Moby Dick, Jungle Book: Stories, Understanding Comics, The Tale of One Bad Rat,* and *Pedro and Me.*

3.3.7 Summary

- Graphic novels can help students develop literacy skills by reinforcing language and vocabulary.
- Graphic novels rely on text density as well as their number of pages to accurately reflect their literacy value.
- Graphic novels are real books that use traditional literary devices to tell the story.
- Discussions of graphic novels can encourage critical thinking skills.
- Interpreting graphic novels can help students develop visual literacy skills.

4

Core Titles Listing

4.1 THINGS TO CONSIDER

It is by intent that the list of core titles in this chapter is somewhat conservative. Items that are popular in one community may not be successful in another, so this resource is designed for both public and school libraries, two agencies that have slightly different goals and clientele.

There are many "Best Graphic Novels for Libraries" books and Web sites available. Vendors and library associations are joining the cause, endeavoring to promote their materials as "the best." This list is not meant to represent the best—that designation is almost impossible in a field that is still evolving. Instead, this core collection contains old standards and new classics that will do your collection proud.

A reminder on the topic of series development: Consider starting with the earliest volume available and work your way up. If money is no object, purchase the entire set. Otherwise, purchase in groups of three or four volumes. That is enough to maintain a reader's interest and desire for "what's next?" without investing hundreds of dollars in a series that may have limited interest. So, for series: Purchase small quantities, and purchase regularly.

Develop the collection in all genres. You may find that Manga and superheroes are incredibly popular at your facility. Be sure to acquire more titles in these areas, but do not neglect the other topics necessary to round out a graphic novel collection.

This core titles listing will get new collections started with the most recommended and most accepted titles for graphic novels in public and school libraries. Remember, always preview titles, collect reviews, and purchase new series sparingly.

4.2 STARTING OUT

This type of collection is ideal for libraries with no graphic novels whatsoever. It is well rounded and can be used to test market a GN collection. Note: all prices are current, spring 2004.

Busiek, Kurt, and Alex Ross. 1999. *Marvels*. New York: Marvel Comics (ISBN: 0–78510–049–0). $19.95.

Everyday citizens have a different view of superheroes. Amid falling rubble and colossal explosions, a reporter tries to piece together the real story of what is happening to his city. Superheroes for teens.

DC Comics. 1993. *The Death of Superman*. New York: DC Comics (ISBN: 1–56389–097–6). $6.95.

Part of the "death and rebirth of Superman" saga, readers learn how the most powerful hero of all time is defeated, and what he died to defend. Superheroes for all ages.

DC Comics. 1993. *The World without Superman*. New York: DC Comics (ISBN: 1–56389–118–2). $7.50.

The middle segment of the "death and rebirth of Superman" saga. Superheroes for teens.

Eisner, Will. 2001. *The Princess and the Frog*. New York: NBM Publishing (ISBN: 1–56163–244–9). $15.95.

Golden, Christopher. 1999. *Buffy the Vampire Slayer: The Origin*. Milwaukie, OR: Dark Horse Comics (ISBN: 1–56971–429–0). $9.95.

Based on the television series, Golden's work showcases a young woman with an ordinary life who learns she is destined for something greater. Horror for teens.

Hosler, Jay. 2000. *Clan Apis*. Columbus, OH: Active Synapse (ISBN: 0–967–72550–X). $15.00.

Through comic art and humor, Hosler give us the honeybee's life and environment. Nonfiction for all ages.

McCloud, Scott. 1994. *Understanding Comics*. New York: HarperPerennial (ISBN: 0–06097–625–X). $22.95.

At times existential, McCloud takes the reader through the physical and psychological means and methods of what a comic is and how it works. A brilliant self-referential treatise on comic art. Nonfiction for teens.

Pini, Wendy, and Richard Pini. *Elfquest: Readers Collection* (**series**). Poughkeepsie, NY: Wolfrider Books.

1999. *Vol. 1, Fire & Flight* (ISBN: 0–93686–155–X). $11.95.

1999. *Vol. 2, Forbidden Grove* (ISBN: 0–93686–156–8). $11.95.

1999. *Vol. 3, Captives of Blue Mountain* (ISBN: 0–93686–157–6). $11.95.

1999. *Vol. 4, Quest's End* (ISBN: 0–93686–158–4). $11.95.

1999. *Vol. 5, Siege at Blue Mountain* (ISBN: 0–93686–159–2). $11.95.

1999. *Vol. 6, Secret of Two-Edge* (ISBN: 0–93686–160–6). $11.95.

1999. *Vol. 7, Cry from Beyond* (ISBN: 0–93686–161–4). $11.95.

and more . . .

In another time and place, the Wolfriders could have lived peacefully with the evolving humans. If only their own kind would cooperate. This massive epic follows sylvan elves on a journey to discover their origins and reaches into the distant future of both species. Fantasy for teens.

Russell, P. Craig. 2003. ***Jungle Book: Stories***. New York: NBM Publishing, Inc. (ISBN: 1–561–63152–3). $16.95.

Russell's stylistic nouveau artwork breathes emotion and depth into the last chapters of Kipling's *Jungle Book,* doing suitable justice to the classic. A classic for all ages.

Smith, Jeff. ***Bone*** (series). Columbus, OH: Cartoon Books.

1994. *Out from Boneville* (ISBN: 0–96366–090–X). $12.95.

1994. *Great Cow Race* (ISBN: 0–96366–092–6). $12.95.

1996. *Eyes of the Storm* (ISBN: 0–96366–096–9). $16.95.

1999. *The Dragonslayer* (ISBN: 1–88896–300–X). $16.95.

1999. *Rock Jaw: Master of the Eastern Border* (ISBN: 1–88896–303–4). $14.95.

1999. *Old Man's Cave* (ISBN: 1–88896–305–0). $12.95.

"Pogo meets Tolkien" when the Bone cousins are run out of town on a rail and land in small village that stands between ancient evil and its control of the world. Fantasy for all ages.

Spiegelman, Art. 2000. ***Little Lit: Folklore and Fairy Tale Funnies***. New York: Joanna Colter (ISBN: 0–06028–624–5). $19.95.

Spiegelman, Art. 1986. ***Maus: A Survivor's Tale*** (***My Father Bleeds History***) [***Vol.1***]. New York: Pantheon (ISBN: 0–394–74723–2). $14.00.

1991. *Vol. II, And Here My Troubles Began* (ISBN: 0–67972–977–1). $14.00.

The stark horrors of the Holocaust are tempered by rich family history as Vladek Spiegelman and his wife Anna are drawn into a terrible chapter in the world's history. Nonfiction for teens.

Talbot, Bryan. 1995. ***The Tale of One Bad Rat***. Milwaukie, OR: Dark Horse Comics (ISBN: 1–56971–077–5). $14.95.

After being sexually abused by her father, Helen Potter travels the cities and countryside of England on a journey of healing. Talbot tactfully handles this sensitive story. Drama for teens.

Tolkien, J.R.R., Charles Dixon (ed.), David Wenzel (illus.). 1991. ***The Hobbit: Graphic Novel***. New York: HarperCollins Publishers (ISBN: 0–261–10266–4). $12.95.

From the idyllic Shire of the Hobbits, through the dark gloom of Murkwood, Wenzel aptly capture the spirit and mood of Tolkien's Middle Earth. A fantasy for teens.

Veitch, Tom, and Cam Kennedy. ***Star Wars: Dark Empire*** (**series**). Milwaukie, OR: Dark Horse Comics.

1995. *Dark Empire, Vol.1* (ISBN: 1–56971–073–2). $17.95.
1995. *Dark Empire, Vol. 2* (ISBN: 1–56971–194–4). $17.95.

After the Empire is fragmented, Luke Skywalker begins his fall to the Dark Side of the Force. Science fiction for all ages.

Waid, Mark, and Alex Ross. 1997. ***Kingdom Come***. New York: DC Comics (ISBN: 1–56389–330–4). $14.95.

This alternate future is a dark place for humans and heroes alike, as self-appointed meta-humans display their deadly powers with little regard for peace or life. Almost every hero in the DC Comics universe must choose sides for the coming final battle. Superheroes for teens.

Williams, Marcia. 1998. ***The Illiad and the Odyssey***. Boston: Candlewick Press (ISBN: 0–76360–644–8). $7.99.

4.3 SMALL AND GROWING

Once a small collection has demonstrated its worth in terms of circulation or in its cultural or educational value, these additional titles are recommended to expand its use and value.

Busiek, Kurt, and Brent Anderson. 2000. ***Kurt Busiek's Astro City: Life in the Big City***. New York: DC Comics (ISBN: 1–56389–551–X). $19.95.

Busiek's new breed of superheroes shows that not all heroes are larger than life, and that the human side must come first. Superheroes for teens.

Delgado, Richard. 1997. ***Age of Reptiles: The Hunt***. Milwaukie, OR: Dark Horse Comics (ISBN: 1–56971–199–2). $17.95.

Splendid artwork is the only tool Delgado uses to show the lives and times of dinosaurs. Bloody at times, the wordless story conveys the adventures and tragedies of prehistory. Fiction for all ages.

Ellis, Warren. 2003. *Orbiter*. New York: DC Comics (ISBN: 1–4012–0056–7). $24.95.

Ten years after it disappeared, a space shuttle comes home—with only one crewmember and filled with alien technology. Science fiction for teens.

Kahan, Bob. 1993. *Return of Superman*. New York: DC Comics (ISBN: 1–56389–149–2). $14.95.

This definitive volume covers the end of the "death and rebirth of Superman" saga, including the fate of the imposters who attempted to take his place. Superheroes for all ages.

Medley, Linda. *Castle Waiting*. Colombus, OH: Olio Press/Cartoon Books.

1994. *The Curse of Brambly Hedge* (ISBN: 0–96518–521–4). $9.95.
2003. *The Lucky Road* (ISBN: 0–96518–523–0). $17.95.

Fantasy and fairy tales abound with a few twists in Medley's storybook wonderland. Stories that show classic fairy tales from the inside and leave you wondering "what if?" Fantasy for teens.

Melville, Herman, and Will Eisner. 2003. *Moby Dick*. New York: NBM Publishing, Inc. (ISBN: 1–561–63294–5). $7.95.

A brief adaptation of the classic human obsession tale. Classic for all ages.

Miller, Frank. 2002. *Daredevil Visionaries: Frank Miller, Vol. 1*. New York: Marvel Comics (ISBN: 0–7851–0757–6). $17.95.

Classic daredevil tales from the early comics show how Matt Murdock, blind attorney by day, acrobatic superhero at night, battles unforgettable characters such as the Kingpin, Bullseye, and Electra, the woman Matt loves but is forced to oppose. Superheroes for all ages.

Morrison, Grant. 2000. *JLA: Earth 2*. New York: DC Comics (ISBN: 1–56389–575–7). $24.95.

One of the best *Justice League* stories available, *Earth 2* is an "anti-Earth," where the alter egos of Superman, Wonder Woman, Aquaman, and the rest are as destructive as our own heroes are beneficent. Superheroes for teens.

Ottaviani, Jim. 2000. *Dignifying Science*. Ann Arbor, MI: G.T. Labs (ISBN: 0–96601–061–2). $16.95.

Biographical stories of female scientists, drawn by a cadre of women artists, profile Rosalind Franklin, Lise Mietner, Hedy Lamarr, and others. Nonfiction for teens.

Takeuchi, Naoko. ***Sailor Moon SuperS*** **(series)**. Los Angeles, CA: Mixx Entertainment, Inc.

> 2003. *Vol. 1* (ISBN: 1–89221–312–5). $9.95.
> 2003. *Vol. 2* (ISBN: 1–89221–324–9). $9.95.

Modern mythology, this companion series to the anime/videos takes the beloved heroines on adventures through space, time, and their hearts. Manga for teens.

Thompson, Jill. ***Scary Godmother*** **(series)**. San Antonio, TX: Sirius Entertainment.

> 1997. *Vol. 1* (ISBN: 1–57989–015–6). $19.95.
> 1998. *Vol. II: The Revenge of Timmy* (ISBN: 1–57989–020–2). $19.95.
> 1999. *Vol. III: The Mystery Date* (ISBN: 1–57989–026–1). $19.95.

While Hannah is trick-or-treating, her cousin plans to scare her when she returns home. Little does he know that Hannah has found her Scary Godmother on that dark night and returns home with the help of a host of creepy creatures. Fiction for all ages.

4.4 TITLES EVERY COLLECTION "SHOULD" HAVE

These titles can be considered required holdings, but are not necessarily needed as initial purchases. They complement other items in the collection and allow existing collections to show the diversity of graphic storytelling.

Avi. 1995. ***City of Light, City of Dark***. New York: Orchard Books (ISBN: 0–53107–058–1). $8.99.
   A timeless tale that takes two youths on an adventure to find the lost power source of a forgotten people that controls the day, night, and seasons of a human metropolis. Fantasy for all ages.

Boyd, Robert F., and Robert L. Fleming. 1995. ***Big Book of Urban Legends***. New York: DC Comics (ISBN: 1–56389–165–4). $19.95.
   A collection of apocryphal stories of modern myth drawn by various artists. Nonfiction for teens.

Eisner, Will. 2000. ***A Contract with God***. New York: DC Comics (ISBN: 1–56389–674–5). $12.95.
   Eisner shows the human condition with artfully crafted stories and detailed artwork as he tells stories from his youth in a Bronx tenement. First-ever graphic novel printed in original book form—not a collection of bound serials. Drama for teens.

Gaiman, Neil. 1993. *The Books of Magic*. New York: DC Comics (ISBN: 1–56389–082–8). $19.95.

A history of magic seen from a young boy's point of view, Gaiman weaves together loose threads of the DC Comics universe to show a young mage what to do, and what not to do. Fantasy for teens.

Gaiman, Neil. *Sandman* (series). New York: DC Comics.

> 1990. *Vol. I: Preludes & Nocturnes* (ISBN: 1–56389–011–9). $19.95.
> 1991. *Vol. II: Doll's House* (ISBN: 0–93028–959–5). $19.95.
> 1991. *Vol. III: Dream Country* (ISBN: 1–56389–016–X). $14.95.
> 1992. *Vol. IV: Season of Mists* (ISBN: 1–56389–041–0). $19.95.
> 1993. *Vol. V: A Game of You* (ISBN: 1–56389–089–5). $19.95.
> and more . . .

In Dream, nothing is what is seems, but running the Dreaming is not easy for the Sandman, and his relatives Death and Delirium can sometimes do little but offer moral support. Horror for teens.

Gonick, Larry. 1997. *Cartoon History of the Universe: Vols. 1–7*. New York: Doubleday (ISBN: 0–38526–520–4). $21.95.

An informative history of the planet, from the big bang through evolving hominids. Nonfiction for all ages.

Goscinny, René. 2004. *Asterix the Gaul*. London: Orion Books (ISBN: 0–75286–605–5). $9.95.

Millions of copies of the Asterix stories have been sold worldwide, telling the adventures of Asterix, the Gaul, in 50 B.C. Filled with historical tidbits, Latin puns, and funny characters that will appeal to children and adults, *Maximum Asterix* brings together "Asterix and the Black Gold," "Asterix and Son," "Operation Getafix," "Asterix and the Magic Carpet," and "Asterix and Obelix all at Sea." Fiction for all ages.

Hergé. *The Adventures of Tintin, Vol. 1*. Little, Brown & Co. (ISBN: 0–31635–940–8). $17.95.

Three of the classic stories are bound in this volume: *Tintin in America, Cigars of the Pharaoh*, and *The Blue Lotus*. A product of their times, the stories contain well thought-out characters and detailed artwork. Fiction for all ages.

Kubert, Joe. 1996. *Fax from Sarajevo*. Milwaukie, OR: Dark Horse Comics (ISBN: hardcover, 1–56971–143–7; paperback, 1–56971–346–4). $16.95.

Kubert crafts a haunting and memorable tale, built on actual faxes received from a family trapped in the siege of Sarajevo. Nonfiction for teens.

Miyazaki, Hayao. 1995–1999. *Nausicaa of the Valley of the Wind*. San Francisco, CA: Viz Communications.

> *Perfect Collection I* (ISBN: 1–56931–096–3). $17.95.
> *Perfect Collection II* (ISBN: 1–56931–087–4). $17.95.
> *Perfect Collection III* (ISBN: 1–56931–111–0). $17.95.
> *Perfect Collection IV* (ISBN: 1–56931–211–7). $17.95.
> and more . . .

This Manga epic shows a young woman's journey to hold her country together in a time of war by being both its princess and its savior. Manga for teens.

Ottaviani, Jim. 2001. *Fallout: J. Robert Oppenheimer, Leo Szilard, and the Political Science of the Atomic Bomb*. Ann Arbor, MI: G.T. Labs (ISBN: 0–96601–063–9). $19.95.

Fallout shows the lives of Oppenheimer and Szilard as they work on super-secret government research: the Manhattan Project. Later chapters are lavishly detailed with Oppenheimer's letters. Nonfiction for teens.

Sacco, Joe. 2002. *Palestine*. Seattle, WA: Fantagraphics Books (ISBN: 1–56097–432–X). $22.95.

Based on his research on the West Bank and the Gaza Strip, Sacco presents a piece of political and historical nonfiction that earned him the title "comic book journalist." Nonfiction for teens.

Takahashi, Rumiko. 1993–1999. *Ranma ½ (series)*. San Francisco, CA: Viz Communications.

> *Vol. I* (ISBN: 0–92927–993–X). $16.95.
> *Vol. II* (ISBN: 1–56931–016–5). $15.95.
> *Vol. III* (ISBN: 1–56931–020–3). $15.95.
> *Vol. IV* (ISBN: 1–56931–085–8). $15.95.
> and more . . .

After an accident at a cursed spring, young Ranma finds that he changes gender when exposed to water. A kung fu Manga comedy for teens.

Winick, Judd. 2000. *Pedro and Me: Friendship, Loss, and What I Learned*. Henry Holt (ISBN: 0–80506–403–6). $16.00.

MTV's *The Real World* highlighted an irrepressible young man, Pedro Zamora, who fought and lost his battle with AIDS. Winick, Pedro's roommate during the third season of the show, paints a poignant and memorable look at Pedro's life and work. Drama for teens.

4.5 SECONDARY PURCHASES

Aragones, Sergio. 1999. ***Groo: The Most Intelligent Man in the World.***
Milwaukie, OR: Dark Horse Comics (ISBN: 1–56971–294–8). $9.95.
   This Eisner-award winning artist shows what happens when a barbarian
with the lowest IQ in the world starts passing out advice. Humor for all ages.

Fijishima, Kosuke. ***Oh My Goddess!*** **(series)**. Milwaukie, OR: Dark Horse
Comics.

   2003. *Traveler* (ISBN: 1–56971–986–1). $17.95.
   2002. *Queen Sayoko* (ISBN: 1–56971–766–4). $16.95.
   2002. *Final Exam* (ISBN: 1–56971–765–6). $13.95.

Episodic stories tell the story of student Keiichi Morisato's life with Bell-
dandy, a goddess. Through his mundane earthly existence of school and
friends, Keiichi's life takes unpredictable twists when other goddesses try to
help him. Manga for teens.

Various. ***DC Archives*** **(series)**. New York: DC Comics.

   2003. *Batman Archives, Vol. 1* (ISBN: 1–56389–932–9). $49.95.
   1998. *Flash Archives, Vol. 1* (ISBN: 1–56389–139–5). $49.95.
   1999. *Green Lantern Archives, Vol. 1* (ISBN: 1–56389–507–2). $49.95.

Collections of early stories in the DC superhero universe, these titles (like
the *Marvel Masterworks* series) are excellent choices to support newer superhero GNs. Superheroes for all ages.

Various. ***Marvel Masterworks*** **(series)**. New York: Marvel Comics.

   2002. *Spider-Man, Vol. 1* (ISBN: 0–78510–864–5). $49.95.
   2003. *Fantastic Four, Vol. 3* (ISBN: 0–78511–182–4). $49.95.
   2003. *Avengers, Vol. 1* (ISBN: 0–78510–883–1). $49.95.

Considered secondary purchases because of price, these bound collections
are worthwhile additions to a GN collection. They supplement the storylines
of newer superhero graphic novels by providing the original stories, which involved many familiar characters. Superheroes for all ages.

5

Finding the Best of Graphic Novels

5.1 BEST-SELLING GRAPHIC NOVELS

What's hot and what's not changes from month to month, season to season. Therefore, a reliable place to turn for advice on the continually evolving state of graphic novels are the industry's best-sellers lists. One source for industry news is www.icv2.com, which tracks the retailing of comic and graphic novel publications, media, and toys.

The table *Tip of the Top* lists best-selling graphic novels from this site's monthly "top 10" lists, information reprinted by permission from Icv2.com. Reflecting a period of six months, the information is organized by each title's rank on the listing. All of the first-place titles are listed first, the second-place titles next, and so on. Within each ranking, the titles are alphabetized. A few notable trends can be observed:

- **More than half the graphic novels are in the superhero genre.** Of those, 44 percent have strong media tie-ins, such as movies or television programs.
- **10 percent of the titles are Manga.** As is typical of this genre, all are part of series.
- **Classic children's comic characters are well represented:** 8 percent of the titles are based on Walt Disney characters or Charles Schultz's *Peanuts* comic strip.
- **60 percent of the titles are volumes of a series.** Thirty-six of the sixty titles surveyed are components of a series, while the remainder are stand-alone graphic novels. 58 percent of the series titles are within the first three volumes of a new series.

What does this data from the comic book industry mean for a public or school library? Can every title on the list be ordered? Would a library have to acquire all the titles for a well-rounded collection?

Firstly, these top-10 lists represent *retail* sales to the general public. They may be biased toward adults or collectors and not necessarily reflect the reading interests of children and teens. That said, not every title may be appropriate for a library collection, particularly for graphic novel collections shelved in a children's area. The superhero genre is both popular and, quite often, safe for teens. Manga is very well represented on the best-sellers list and can be extremely popular in some libraries, even though some titles are inappropriate for children. It is always recommended to preview titles before purchase.

Children's comic characters such as Donald Duck or Charlie Brown should be considered for acquisition. They are both surprisingly popular in retail and are worthwhile additions to a graphic novel collection that is available to school-aged readers.

On the subject of series, one recommendation is to purchase only a few titles at a time. This allows your library to evaluate the success of a series at your location as well as build suspense for your patrons as they wait for the next installment. Consider budgeting the cost of a larger series over a two-year period. This breaks the purchase into small, manageable batches, while ensuring that the full set is being acquired.

Graphic Novels Sales Rise

In 2002, over $50 million of graphic novels and comics were sold in America.
In 2003, over $160 million titles were sold.
Sales in 2004 are estimated to show another 80 percent increase: over $280 million!

Top Genres in 2004

Three genres topped the charts in the first half of 2004: superhero, horror, and Manga. The lowest-selling categories were fantasy, nonfiction, and drama. Several genres of graphic novels did not even appear on the top-10 charts during the survey period—mysteries, science fiction, classics, and general fiction books.

Top Characters

Three characters appeared in the most graphic novels during the first six months of 2004: Spider-Man, Batman, and Donald Duck.

	Tip of the Top: Best-Selling Graphic Novels (Jan.–June 2004)		
Place in Top 10	Title	Price	Month
1	New X-Men Vol 6 Planet X TP	12.99	February-04
1	Spawn Simony	7.95	May-04
1	Superman Red Son TP	17.95	January-04
1	Ultimate Spider-Man Vol 9 Ultimate Six TP	17.99	June-04
1	Ultimates Vol 2 Homeland Security TP	17.99	March-04
1	Y the Last Man Vol 3 One Small Step TP	12.95	April-04
2	Essential Punisher Vol 1 TP	14.99	February-04
2	Essential Spider-Man Vol 6 TP	16.99	June-04
2	Superman/Batman Public Enemies HC	19.95	March-04
2	Teen Titans Kids Game TP	9.95	April-04
2	Trigun Vol 2 TP	14.95	January-04
2	Ultimate Spider-Man Vol 8 Cats & Kings TP	17.99	May-04
3	Donald Duck Adventures Vol 4 TP	7.95	February-04
3	Fables Vol 3 Storybook Love TP	14.95	March-04
3	Supreme Power Vol 1 Contact TP	14.99	April-04
3	Ultimate X-Men Vol 7 Blockbuster TP	12.99	January-04
3	Walt Disney's Vacation Parade	8.95	June-04
3	Witchblade/Darkminds Return of Paradox TP	9.99	May-04
4	Chronicles of Conan Vol 4 Red Nails & Other Stories TP	15.95	May-04
4	Chronicles of Conan Vol 3 Monoliths & Stories TP	15.95	January-04
4	Dark Horse Book of Witchcraft HC	14.95	June-04
4	Formerly Known as Justice League TP	12.95	April-04
4	Hellsing Vol 2 TP	13.95	March-04
4	Lovecraft HC	24.95	February-04

Place in Top 10	Title	Price	Month
5	Essential Tomb of Dracula Vol 2 TP	16.99	March-04
5	Hellboy Vol 1 Seed of Destruction TP	17.95	April-04
5	Hellsing Vol 3 TP	13.95	June-04
5	JLA Zatannas Search TP	12.95	January-04
5	Thor Vikings TP	13.99	February-04
5	Transmetropolitan Vol 10 One More Time TP	14.95	May-04
6	Batman Illustrated by Neal Adams Vol 2 HC	49.95	June-04
6	Berserk Vol 3 TP	13.95	March-04
6	Born HC	17.99	February-04
6	New X-Men Vol 7 Here Comes Tomorrow	10.99	May-04
6	Outsiders Looking For Trouble TP	12.95	January-04
6	Planetary Crossing Worlds TP	14.95	April-04
7	Batman I/Forties TP	19.95	April-04
7	Berzerk Vol 2 Guardians of Desire TP	13.95	January-04
7	Complete Peanuts Vol 1 1950-1952 HC	28.95	May-04
7	Essential Daredevil Vol 2 TP	16.99	March-04
7	Rurouni Kenshin Vol 3 GN	7.95	February-04
7	Spider-Man 2 movie TP	12.99	June-04
8	Amazing Spider-Man Vol 6 Happy Birthday TP	12.99	April-04
8	Arkham Asylum Living Hell TP	12.95	February-04
8	Catwoman Nine Lives of Feline Fatale	14.95	June-04
8	Dark Days TP	19.99	March-04
8	Global Frequency Planet Ablaze TP	14.95	January-04
8	Trigun Maximum Vol 1 Hero Returns TP	9.95	May-04
9	Donald Duck Adventures Vol 5 TP	7.95	April-04

Place in Top 10	Title	Price	Month
9	Hellboy Vol 1 Seed of Destruction TP	17.95	March-04
9	MegaTokoyo Vol 2 TP	9.95	January-04
9	Rurouni Kenshin Vol 5 GN	7.95	June-04
9	Walking Dead Vol 1 Days Gone Bye TP	9.95	May-04
9	Wonder Woman Gods & Mortals TP	19.95	February-04
10	Birds of Prey of Like Minds TP	14.95	February-04
10	CSI Miami Thou Shalt Not	6.99	May-04
10	Donald Duck Adventures Vol 6 TP	7.95	June-04
10	Liberty Meadows Vol 2 Creature Comforts HC	24.95	January-04
10	Mighty Love HC	24.95	April-04
10	Rurouni Kenshin Vol 4 GN	7.95	March-04

Source: "Top Graphic Novels" lists, Jan. 04–June 04, www.icv2.com.

5.2 COMIC ART GLOSSARY

Comic art is a distinct form of storytelling. Just as audios and videos differ from text novels, comic art expresses information in a unique, visual way.

This format has four main categories: cartoons, comic strips, comic books, and graphic novels. Generally acknowledged as beginning in the 1970s, graphic novels are a relatively recent development in the comic arts family. This modern form of visual storytelling has a history that, beginning with single images, has grown into a complex medium.

Type: Cartoons. The basis of the art form.

Definition: cartoon. Defined as a humorous or satirical drawing. Note that when *cartoon* refers to animation, the definition is still valid. To animate, the illustrations are drawn individually on single sheets of clear plastic called cels. Characters are shown in slightly different poses in each picture. When the cels are photographed and shown in sequence, the illusion of motion is generated.

Description: A cartoon is a single panel of comic art. The images seldom express literal action, focusing instead on conveying a concept. The panel should have both an image and text. The text is often spoken within a speech balloon by a character, although it may be printed in a caption.

Type: Comic Strips. The basis of the phenomenon.

Definition: comic strip. Defined as a sequence of cartoons that relates a narrative story. The key here is that the drawings are in a specific sequence that tells a story.

Description: A comic strip can be recognized by its distinctive series of panels that blend art and text. Comic strips always express the narrative or literal action of their characters, often expressing both. Comic strips can be evaluated as a series of panels describing a single scene.

Type: Comic Books. The basis of the story.

Definition: comic book. Defined as sequences of comic strips, often relating a single story, bound as a magazine. Although a comic book contains collections of comic strips, this does not constitute a graphic novel. A comic book is properly categorized as a serial.

Description: Identify comic art as a comic book if it has many pages filled with artistic panels that express the mood and action of a storyline. Episodic by nature, this species of comic art often ends with a cliffhanger. Consider it a series of scenes that describe a single episode. The wordless variety is almost nonexistent, except for very special issues of the most popular titles.

Type: Graphic Novels. The pinnacle of comic art.

Definition: graphic novel. Defined as a book presenting a fictional story told in a comic-strip format. Following this boiler-plate definition, collections of comic strips (such as *Garfield*) would be on par with great graphic novels such as Art Spiegelman's Pulitzer Prize-winning book, *Maus.* This is patently ridiculous—*Garfield,* while certainly popular, has no place in a graphic novel collection (nor is it Pulitzer-caliber).

Description: A book that expresses a single story through comic art. True GNs tell a continuous story, usually original, expressed through panelized artwork. In the strictest sense, and this is a gray area, graphic novels are not bound collections. A graphic novel was intended, from conception, to be a single work and to be published as such. The fine line between graphic novel and bound collection is often blurred—minute differences between an original graphic novel with chapters and a bound collection with episodes rapidly degenerates into semantics. For practical purposes, however, it is common to refer to *either* of these forms of comic art as graphic novels.

5.3 RESOURCES AND SUGGESTED READING

Abel, Jessica. "The Art of Selling Graphic Novels." *Publisher's Weekly,* June 25, 2001: 18.

Bruggeman, Lora. "Zap! Whoosh! Kerplow!" *School Library Journal,* January 1997: 22.

"Comic Art and Graffix Gallery Virtual Museum: History of Comic Art" (July 2003). Available online at www.comic-art.com/history.htm (accessed January 3, 2005).

"Comic Books: a Research Guide." New York: New York Public Library Humanities and Social Science Library (March 2003). Available online at www.nypl.org/research/chss/grd/resguides/comic/ (accessed January 3, 2005).

"Comics2Film" (June 2003). Available online at www.comics2film.com (accessed January 3, 2005).

DeCandido, Keith R. A. "Picture This: Graphic Novels in Libraries." *Library Journal,* March 1990: 50.

Eisner, Will. 1985. *Comics and Sequential Art.* Tamarac, FL: Poorhouse Press.

Gorman, Michele. "What Teens Want." *School Library Journal,* August 1, 2002: 42.

Lavin, Michael. "Comic Books and Graphic Novels for Libaries: What to Buy." *Serials Review,* Summer 1998: 31.

"The Librarian's Guide to Anime and Manga." Available online at www. koyagi.com/Libguide.html (accessed January 3, 2005).

McCloud, Scott. "Comics and the Visual Revolution." *Publisher's Weekly,* October 11, 1993: 47–53.

McCloud, Scott. 1998. *Understanding Comics.* Northampton, MA: Kitchen Sink Press.

Michigan State University Library Comic Art Collection Reading Room. Available online at http://www.lib.msu.edu/comics/rri/ (accessed January 3, 2005).

New York Comic Book Museum (July 2003). Available online at www. nyccomicbookmuseum.org/education/education.htm (accessed January 3, 2005).

Sabin, Roger. 1996. *Comics, Comix and Graphic Novels: A History of Comic Art.* London: Phaidon Press Ltd.

St. Lifer, Evan. "Graphic Novels, Seriously." *School Library Journal,* August 2002: 9.

Walters, Suzanne. 2004. *Library Marketing That Works.* New York: Neal-Schuman.

Weiner, Stephen. "Beyond Superheroes: Comics Get Serious." *Library Journal,* February 2002: 55.

Weiner, Stephen. "Creating a Graphic Novel Collection for the Public Library." *Voice of Youth Advocates,* December 1992: 270–272.

Wolk, Douglas. "Graphic Novel Sales Even Better Than Reported." *Publisher's Weekly,* June 2004: 18.

Wolk, Douglas. "The Manga Are Coming." *Publisher's Weekly,* May 2002: 29.

THE GRAPHIC NOVELS IN LIBRARIES (GNLIB-L) E-MAIL DISCUSSION LIST

To stay abreast of how others are using and collecting graphic novels, join the Graphic Novels in Libraries (GNLIB-L) e-mail discussion list.

New members should subscribe and spend a few days "lurking" (watching the discussions before participating). What topics are being discussed? Do people reply to every message? Is there any information being presented that can help you with your situation? After you get a feel for the group, dive in with your own questions, and help by sharing your own insights!

To subscribe, send a blank message to gnlib-l-subscribe@topica.com from the e-mail account at which you wish to receive the messages.

To post a message, send the e-mail to gnlib-l@topica.com. Your message will be forwarded to all list subscribers.

The support Web site is located at http://www.angelfire.com/gnlib.

MORE ONLINE RESOURCES

Archives of PUBYAC (Public YA/Children's Librarians): www.pallasinc.com/pubyac/Archives.htm.

Comic Scholars' Discussion List: www.english.ufl.edu/comics/scholars. (Academic forum about research and teaching related to comic art.)

The Comics Get Serious: www.rationalmagic.com/Comics/KidFriendly.html. (Reviews of GNs for teens.)

Grand Comic Book Database: www.comics.org. (Simple database of creator credits, story details, and other useful information.)

Graphic Novels in Education (GNIE-L): www.topica.com/lists/GNIE-L. (Companion list to GNLIB-L; focuses on the use of GNs in K–12 classrooms.)

No Flying, No Tights: www.noflyingnotights.com. (Reviews of GNs for grade-school children.)

Sidekicks: sidekicks.noflyingnotights.com. (Reviews of GNs for children.)

5.4 GRAPHIC NOVEL AND COMIC PUBLISHERS

Some of the most popular publishers in the comics industry are mentioned below. Visit their Web sites, if possible, to get an idea of their services and publications. Not all material published by these companies will be appropriate for your collection.

CrossGen Entertainment, Inc.
4023 Tampa Road, Suite 2400
Oldsmar, FL 34677
Web site: www.crossgen.com
E-mail: info@crossgen.com

Dark Horse Comics, Inc.
10956 SE Main Street
Milwaukie, OR 97222
Web site: www.darkhorse.com

DC Comics
1700 Broadway
New York, NY 10019
Phone: 212-636-5400
Orders: 800-759-0190
Web site: www.dccomics.com

Image Comics
1071 N. Batavia Street, Suite A
Orange, CA 92867
Phone: 714-288-0200
E-mail: info@imagecomics.com

Marvel Enterprises, Inc.
10 East 40th Street
New York, NY 10016
Web site: www.marvel.com
Subscriptions: 1-800-217-9158

Viz Shop-by-Mail
P.O. Box 77010
San Francisco, CA 94107
Phone: 1-800-394-3042

Titles, Series, and Characters Index

Author and Illustrator Index

General Index

About the Author

Steve Miller has worked in public and school libraries in northeastern Ohio for more than a decade. He is the creator of acclaimed online resources for public and school librarians: the Graphic Novels in Libraries (GNLIB-L), Teen Advisory Groups Advisors' Discussion (TAGAD-L), and Graphic Novels in Education (GNIE-L) e-mail discussion groups. Mr. Miller has presented workshops guiding nonprofit organizations in the creation of private library collections, and he has worked with libraries on creating and managing teen advisory groups (TAGs).